T0312671

THE DOUBLE V CAMPAIGN

THE DOUBLE V CAMPAIGN

*African Americans Fighting for Freedom
at Home and Abroad*

LEA LYON

ROWMAN & LITTLEFIELD
Lanham • Boulder • New York • London

Published by Rowman & Littlefield

An imprint of The Rowman & Littlefield Publishing Group, Inc.

4501 Forbes Boulevard, Suite 200, Lanham, Maryland 20706

www.rowman.com

86-90 Paul Street, London EC2A 4NE, United Kingdom

Cover images credits, clockwise from top left: National Archives; Philadelphia Record Photograph Morgue [V07], Historical Society of Pennsylvania; National Archives; *Pittsburgh Courier* Archives/ *New Pittsburgh Courier.*

British Library Cataloguing in Publication Information available

Library of Congress Cataloging-in-Publication Data Available

ISBN 9781538184653 (cloth : alk. paper) | ISBN 9781538184660 (epub)

♾️™ The paper used in this publication meets the minimum requirements of American National Standard for Information Sciences—Permanence of Paper for Printed Library Materials, ANSI/NISO Z39.48-1992.

Contents

ACKNOWLEDGMENTS

THIS BOOK BEGAN WITH A SUGGESTION FROM BETTY REID Soskin, the popular and revered African American U.S. park ranger who, until her retirement at the age of 100 in 2022, regularly shared her wisdom and experience in talks at the Rosie the Riveter/World War II Home Front National Historical Park in Richmond, California. After one such gathering, I introduced myself to Ms. Soskin and asked her what one children's book *she* would like to see about the World War II era she had just shared. She immediately replied, "The Double V campaign," adding that James G. Thompson, whose letter started it all, was an unsung hero who should be remembered.

Her enthusiasm led me to learn about the Double V campaign, and James Thompson, and the more I researched, the more engrossed I became. Thanks to Betty Reid Soskin for her excitement and support of my project.

A special thank you to my agent Abigail Samoun of Red Fox Literary, who has championed this project throughout, offering excellent editorial advice and enthusiastically submitting it to editors.

I also want to thank Professor Emeritus Patrick S. Washburn of Ohio University. In addition to his two definitive books and three documentaries on the Black press, which were invaluable to me, he generously made himself available to me, guiding me in the right direction for my project.

I located two of James Thompson's relatives who remember him as their father's white-haired first cousin. I so appreciate their assistance and information, including that Thompson's athletic trophies from Wichita High School North were still on display more than 70 years later. Thanks to Cerelia Smith-St. Claire and Sheri Daniel for their interest and help.

And thanks to another expert on the Black press, Earnest L. Perry Jr., PhD, the African American associate dean for graduate studies and research at the University of Missouri School of Journalism, for his enthusiasm about my book.

Finally, I am grateful to my critique group friends for their continued insights and advice as this book developed.

CHRONOLOGY

1939 World War II begins when Adolf Hitler, the Nazi German dictator, orders his army to invade Poland.

1940 The *Pittsburgh Courier* smuggles Black newspapers to the Jim Crow South throughout the war.

1941 January: President Franklin Delano Roosevelt asks manufacturers to switch to building military equipment to help the Allies fight the war, starting the "defense industry." **January 25:** A. Philip Randolph announces his plan for the March on Washington, and the date is set for July 1, 1941. **June 18:** A meeting is held between Randolph and President Roosevelt about the March on Washington. **June 25:** President Roosevelt signs Executive Order 8802 desegregating the defense industry, and the March on Washington is postponed. **July:** The March on Washington Movement continues to fight against discrimination. **September:** Judge William Hastie pushes to end the frequent racial violence at and around army bases. **December 7:** Japan attacks Pearl Harbor; Dorie Miller shoots down four Japanese planes, becoming the first Black hero at Pearl Harbor. **December 8:** The United States declares war on Japan.

1942 **January 15:** James G. Thompson sends his letter to the offices of the *Pittsburgh Courier*. **January 31:** Thompson's letter to the editor is published in the *Courier*. **February:** The government ramps up its investigation of the Black press. **February 7:** The Double V campaign rollout begins. **April:** George S. Schuyler interviews Thompson in Wichita, Kansas; Thompson is hired as director of the *Courier*'s national Double V campaign. **June 1:** The U.S. Navy, Coast Guard, and Marines begin accepting Black recruits for the general service sector. **Mid-June:** A meeting between Francis Biddle and John Sengstacke removes the fear of the government closing down the Black press. **Fall:** The *Courier* begins to phase out mention of the Double V campaign in the newspaper.

1943 **February 10:** James G. Thompson is inducted into the U.S. Army. **November 24:** Dorie Miller dies when the carrier ship *Liscome Bay* sinks.

1944 **March 25:** The first African American officers are commissioned in the U.S. Navy.

1945 **April 12:** President Franklin D. Roosevelt dies of a stroke; Vice President Harry S. Truman becomes president of the United States. **May 8:** Nazi Germany surrenders. **September 2:** Japan surrenders, ending World War II.

1946 **December 5:** Executive Order 9980, signed by President Truman President's Committee on Civil Rights, recommends desegregating the military.

1947 Manager Branch Rickey signs Jackie Robinson as first baseman for the Brooklyn Dodgers.

1948 **July 26:** President Harry Truman signs Executive Order 9981 ordering an end to segregation in the military.

IMPORTANT NAMES

AFL-CIO The AFL (American Federation of Labor) and CIO (Congress of Industrial Organizations) were groups of unions fighting for such economic gains as higher wages, shorter hours, and better conditions for workers. The two organizations merged in 1955 and are still fighting for workers' rights.

Allies The countries Great Britain, the United States, and the Soviet Union, which allied against the Axis powers (Germany, Italy, and Japan) in World War II.

Associated Negro Press A news service supplying Black newspapers with news stories, opinions, columns, feature essays, and coverage of events relevant to black Americans.

Axis powers Germany, Italy, and Japan, fascist countries during World War II.

Bethune, Mary McLeod Member of President Franklin D. Roosevelt's "Black cabinet." Bethune worked in the War Department and was president of the National Council of Negro Women, Inc.

Biddle, Francis B. Attorney general and central player in the fight against the suppression of the Black press.

Black Panthers, 761st Tank Battalion Reached France in October 1944 to serve under General George S. Patton.

Black press Black-owned weekly newspapers throughout the country publishing articles about issues and events important to African Americans.

Bolden, Frank First Black reporter sent overseas by the *Pittsburgh Courier.*

Brotherhood of Sleeping Car Porters Union of the Pullman Porters started by A. Philip Randolph. The first union of African American workers in the country to sign a labor contract with a major corporation.

Cessna Aircraft Company James G. Thompson worked at this company in the cafeteria, because he was Black, until he and others went on strike and he resigned.

Chicago Defender A popular Black newspaper.

Cunningham, Evelyn *Pittsburgh Courier* journalist who specialized in reporting on lynching. Cunningham later had a radio show and was special assistant to Jackie Robinson, then the governor of New York, and President Gerald Ford.

Defense industry President Franklin D. Roosevelt ordered factories everywhere in the country to switch to manufacturing planes, warships, parachutes, and ammunition for the Allied troops in Europe.

Dunnigan, Alice Allison Washington bureau chief for the Associated Negro Press. Dunnigan wrote about politics for 114 Black newspapers. She was the first Black woman accepted into the White House press corps.

Executive Order 8802 Prohibition of Discrimination in the Defense Industry. Signed by the president on June 25, 1941.

Executive Order 9980 Established the multiracial President's Committee on Civil Rights. President Harry S. Truman tasked the committee with studying "how state, federal, and local governments [could] implement the guarantees of personal freedoms embodied in the constitution." Signed on December 5, 1946.

Executive Order 9981 Ordered integration in the military. President Harry S. Truman signed it on July 26, 1948.

Fahy, Charles Former solicitor general appointed by President Harry S. Truman to head a committee to enforce Executive Order 9981 on military desegregation.

Fair Employment Practices Committee (FEPC) Created by Executive Order 8802 to receive and investigate complaints of discrimination and to take appropriate steps to resolve the grievances.

Forrestal, James Secretary of the Navy after Frank Knox. Forrestal opened officer training to larger numbers and at integrated training facilities.

Four freedoms Freedom of speech and expression, freedom of religion, freedom from want, and freedom from fear.

Garland, Phyl *Pittsburgh Courier* journalist.

Golden 13 The first African American men commissioned as officers in the U.S. Navy.

Hastie, William H. Civilian aide to Secretary of War Stimson. Hastie worked to stop racist treatment in the military.

Hoover, J. Edgar FBI director. Hoover tried to stop the Black press.

Ink Spots One of the first Black singing groups popular with both Black and white audiences, with 30 hits on the pop charts, appeared in a photo in the *Pittsburgh Courier* performing "Yankee Doodle Tan." Thompson was singing with them.

Jackson, Juanita Brought 2,000 Black citizens to the capitol of Maryland to calmly protest police brutality in Baltimore.

Jim Crow Laws Set of laws passed in the southern states that imposed racial discrimination and segregation against Black people.

Knox, Frank Secretary of the Navy. Knox was strongly against integrating the U.S. Navy and letting Black sailors be anything other than mess workers.

LaGuardia, Fiorello Mayor of New York City. LaGuardia worked with A. Philip Randolph and Walter White to get Executive Order 8802 passed.

Lane, Layle Lane organized the March on Washington for A. Philip Randolph and led the March on Washington Movement after the march was postponed.

Lewis, Ira Executive editor of the *Pittsburgh Courier.*

Lunceford, Jimmie Famous big-band leader who promoted Double V in shows and radio. Lunceford took Thompson on his first airplane ride.

March on Washington Movement (MOWM) After the 1941 March on Washington was postponed, the committee continued its civil rights work as the MOWM.

Marshall, George C. Army chief of staff.

McKenzie, Edna Chappell Journalist at the *Pittsburgh Courier.*

Miller, Dorie First African American hero at Pearl Harbor.

Murray, Pauli Law student who organized the first nationally recognized "sit-in" at a restaurant.

Myers, E. Pauline Ran the MOWM central office and advocated for active but nonviolent protests.

National Association for the Advancement of Colored People (NAACP) Organization that works to ensure the political, social, and economic equality of all persons and to eliminate racial hatred and racial discrimination through democratic processes. It is the oldest organization of this type.

New Deal   A series of programs, public work projects, and financial reforms enacted by President Franklin D. Roosevelt to provide relief for the needy, economic recovery, and a sense of security during the Great Depression.

Ormes, Jackie   Created comics for the *Pittsburgh Courier* and became the first nationally syndicated African American woman cartoonist.

Patton, George S.   Recognized as the greatest battlefield commander and well-known American general from the modern war era.

Prattis, P. L.   Editor at the *Pittsburgh Courier*. Prattis turned James G. Thompson's letter to the editor into the Double V campaign.

Pullman Porters   Took care of passengers, from carrying luggage to changing seats to beds on Pullman sleeper train cars. They also gathered stories for the *Pittsburgh Courier* and spread the papers to Black communities along their routes. They smuggled the *Courier* into the South.

Randolph, A. Philip   Prominent voice in early civil rights activism. Randolph was a labor unionist who organized and led the Brotherhood of Sleeping Car Porters, the first successful African American labor union. His planned March on Washington led to Executive Order 8802 integrating the defense industry.

Rickey, Branch   Dodgers general manager. Rickey hired Jackie Robinson.

Robinson, Jackie Broke the major league color bar as first Black baseball player since the late 1800s. Robinson was hired by the Brooklyn Dodgers, who appeared in the World Series.

Roosevelt, Eleanor President Franklin D. Roosevelt's wife and First Lady. Eleanor was an activist for equality and helped the home-front effort.

Roosevelt, Franklin D. President of the United States from 1932 and throughout the war until this death in 1945.

Rosie the Riveter Nickname for the many women who were trained to build planes and other military equipment. They filled the jobs of the men who were off fighting in the war.

Rowe, James H., Jr. Assistant to Secretary of State Francis Biddle. Rowe thought of a clever way to distract the president's focus away from the Black press.

Rustin, Bayard Black activist who worked with A. Philip Randolph planning the 1941 March on Washington, later postponed. Rustin later planned Martin Luther King Jr.'s 1963 March on Washington.

Schuyler, George Columnist for the *Pittsburgh Courier*. Schuyler went to Wichita, Kansas, to interview James G. Thompson.

Sengstacke, John L. Publisher of the *Chicago Defender*. Sengstacke met with Secretary of State Biddle to resolve the suppression of the Black press.

Smith, Wendell *Pittsburgh Courier* sportswriter. Smith persuaded the Dodgers to hire Jackie Robinson.

Stevenson, Adlai Convinced Secretary of the Navy Frank Knox to authorize some Black officers. In the 1950s, Stevenson ran for president against Dwight D. Eisenhower.

Stimson, Henry L. Served six presidents from Taft through Truman. Stimson was secretary of war (now secretary of defense) during World War II.

Thompson, James G. Creator of the "Double V" idea, which the *Pittsburgh Courier* turned into a nationwide campaign. Thompson was a young African American civil service worker, freelance journalist, and cafeteria worker in a segregated aircraft factory.

Truman, Harry S. Took over the presidency after President Franklin D. Roosevelt died. He desegregated the military in 1948.

Tuskegee Airmen Team of African American pilots that broke down the barrier for Black pilots and air crews. The Tuskegee Airmen flew more than 15,000 missions during the war, destroyed 261 enemy aircraft, and were awarded more than 850 medals.

Vann, Robert Editor and publisher of the *Pittsburgh Courier*. Vann helped make the *Courier* one of the most popular and successful Black newspapers.

Walker, Frank Postmaster general. Walker tried to block the Black press.

White, Walter   Executive secretary of the NAACP. White led the organization from 1929 to 1955.

Wilkins, Roy   Black activist, journalist, and editor. Wilkins led the NAACP as executive secretary from 1955 to 1971.

Willkie, Wendell   Ran against Roosevelt for president in 1940 and wore a Double V pin on the lapel of his suits.

Women's Army Corps (WAC)   The women's branch of the U.S. Army. Congress ruled that women could enlist in the army doing such jobs as office clerk, cook, truck driver, and messenger to free up more men to fight in the war.

Woodard, Isaac   Black soldier. Woodard was beaten by police when he returned to the South after the war and was blinded. His attack became a driving force in President Harry S. Truman's determination to end racial violence in the country.

INTRODUCTION

THE SECOND WORLD WAR, KNOWN AS WORLD WAR II, HAS been called the largest and most deadly war in history. It lasted from 1939 to 1945 and involved more than 30 countries. Estimates of how many people fought in the war range from 75 million to 128 million, with untold millions of civilians impacted as well.

In the more than 75 years since the war ended, well over 50,000 books have been written and published and almost 5,000 movies produced, relaying many of the events and the experiences of those involved.

But few of these books or movies share the stories of African Americans during this war.

The story of the Double V campaign and what it meant to Black Americans during World War II is one of such hidden narratives. This book sets out to tell the story of how one of the most iconic Black newspapers in America, the *Pittsburgh Courier*, helped its readers understand the importance of supporting the war effort while continuing to fight for equal rights. This offered African Americans an honorable way to fight for freedoms overseas that they didn't experience in America.

I hope that bringing to light this story about African Americans in World War II will help expand our knowledge (and that of young adults) of the complete story of that time and encourage further exploration.

CHAPTER ONE
James G. Thompson

A Dilemma and a Plan

The "V for Victory" sign is being displayed prominently in all so-called democratic countries which are fighting for victory over aggression, slavery, and tyranny. . . . Let Colored[1] Americans adopt the double V for a double victory. The first V for victory over our enemies from without, the second V for victory over our enemies within. For surely those who perpetrate these ugly prejudices here are seeking to destroy our democratic form of government just as surely as the Axis forces.

—JAMES G. THOMPSON, EXCERPT FROM A LETTER TO THE EDITOR, *PITTSBURGH COURIER*, JANUARY 31, 1942, 3

FROM PITTSBURGH, PENNSYLVANIA, TO WICHITA, KANSAS, reporter George Schuyler wondered about the man he was traveling to interview. The 900 miles by plane and train gave him plenty of time to think about James G. Thompson. What sort of person was he?

Schuyler knew that Thompson had a gift with words.[2] That much was clear from the letter he wrote to the Black-owned *Pittsburgh Courier*, Schuyler's newspaper, in which he eloquently expressed a dilemma that he and millions of other African Americans were facing. As much as they wanted to fight for the country they loved, should they risk their lives in a war for freedoms in other nations that they did not have in their own? That decision was unavoidable now that America had officially entered World War II.

Not only was Thompson able to put the problem into words, but he also offered a solution. He suggested African Americans fight two wars at once: against fascism in Europe and Asia and against racism at home. Make the popular "V for Victory" sign with the fingers of both hands: a Double V.

His letter inspired the *Courier* to create a Double V campaign, offering America's Black citizens a way to fight for their own freedoms while fighting for their country.[3]

The response from their readers to Thompson's letter was overwhelming. The *Courier* immediately began publicizing its new campaign with the Double V emblem on every front page. They printed articles about Double V activities around the country. They sold inexpensive Double V badges and buttons to spread the word. Double V clubs sprang up in hundreds of Black communities, sponsoring Double V contests and baseball games, as well as selling bonds to support the war effort.[4] And, with encouragement from the *Courier*, these clubs used the pen, the classroom, and the speaker's platform to oppose racial discrimination at the local level—to fight for their freedoms at home.

Many of the *Courier*'s 1 million readers wrote to the paper wanting to know more about this James G. Thompson, who had given them an elegantly simple way to feel good about fighting for their country. Since the editors did not *know* more about Thompson, they sent George Schuyler to Wichita to meet him.

Now, as he pressed the buzzer at the front door of Thompson's home, Schuyler's curiosity was to be satisfied.[5]

But no one answered the door!

His disappointment changed to delight when a slender, easy-moving, and good-looking man came running toward the house, bounded up the steps to the porch, grasped his hand, and introduced himself as James Thompson.[6] Schuyler was about to have the interview that he had raced through the night and across a half dozen states to get.

"This war is deciding the fate of the world,"[7] Thompson told Schuyler when they had settled in the living room. He explained that, in his opinion, "stopping the Axis dictators from spreading fascism . . . is crucial and will take the strength of *all* Americans working together.

"Our first task, then," he added, "is to fight against discrimination so that a real national unity, a complete national effort may be achieved. As citizens, we should do everything possible to further the efforts of our democracy so that in time it can be, in fact, a REAL democracy."

Schuyler was expecting to meet a young aircraft factory cafeteria worker, as the *Courier* described Thompson. But this serious, intelligent 26-year-old man with a mischievous twinkle in his eye was so much more.

In fact, Schuyler learned, the only reason Thompson was temporarily working in a cafeteria at all was the color of his skin. He had left a challenging and fulfilling civil service job at the Kansas Highway Department to help America produce more military equipment for the war. Because of company policies, Thompson was not allowed to work in the business office or on the factory floor at any of the four aircraft plants in Wichita.[8] He could only be hired to serve food and clean up after the white men who were. So strong was his desire to support his country that he put aside his outrage at this discrimination and accepted a job in the Cessna Aircraft cafeteria.

While working there, he continued to express his ideas and analysis of important things, like segregation and the war, as a freelance newspaper reporter for the Associated Negro Press.[9] His articles were read in various Black newspapers throughout the country.[10]

After a delightful day talking to Thompson and his friends and neighbors in the community, Schuyler raced back to report to the *Courier* what he had discovered.

The *Courier*'s editors, already impressed by Thompson's eloquence and intellect, were thrilled to learn that he was also a government worker and an experienced journalist. They decided to invite him to have a more active part in the campaign.

The momentum sparked by the Double V campaign would continue to grow. It would merge with other efforts to end racial discrimination laying the groundwork for the civil rights movement of the 1950s and 1960s.[11]

A complicated tale was unfolding in America, and the need for national unity had already intensified one day four months earlier, on December 7, 1941, when Japan attacked Pearl Harbor, Hawaii.

CHAPTER TWO

War, Injustice, and a Letter

"Raiders Blast Honolulu, Air and Navy Bases"

Dec. 7—War struck suddenly and without warning from the sky and sea today at the Hawaiian Islands. Japanese bombs took a heavy toll of American lives.
—CHICAGO DAILY TRIBUNE, DECEMBER 8, 1941, 1

"F.D.R. Asks and Signs War Bill within 4 Hours"

Washington, D.C., December 8—President Roosevelt signed a declaration of war against Japan at 3:10 p.m. this afternoon.
—CHICAGO DAILY TRIBUNE, DECEMBER 9, 1941, 1

"YESTERDAY, DECEMBER 7TH, 1941, A DATE WHICH WILL live in infamy, the United States of America was suddenly and deliberately attacked by naval and air forces of the Empire of Japan."[1]

A horrified nation heard these words from President Franklin Delano Roosevelt over the radio. The Pearl Harbor navy base in Hawaii had been bombed. The next day, the United States declared war against Japan and three days later against Germany and Italy, the others in what were known as the Axis countries. America had entered World War II.

Now newspaper headlines and radio bulletins broadcast that thousands of people were enlisting in the armed forces, breaking all recruiting records.

African Americans across the nation were being asked to join a segregated military to fight to restore freedoms in other countries that they didn't have in their own. Should they risk their lives in the name of a democracy that was denied Black citizens?

A serious dilemma, but James G. Thompson was about to change the conversation. He would offer African Americans a symbol and an idea that would inspire and encourage them to fight for their own rights while fighting for their country.

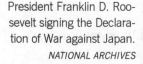
President Franklin D. Roosevelt signing the Declaration of War against Japan.
NATIONAL ARCHIVES

* * *

World War II had begun two years earlier, in 1939, when Adolf Hitler, the Nazi German dictator, ordered his army to invade Poland. Germany now controlled most of Europe, Italy had invaded Africa, and Japan continued its violent expansion into Asia and the Pacific.

These Axis armies and their police forces, mostly Germany's, rounded up, terrorized, and often killed those they considered different and inferior. Not only did the Nazis oppress Jews, but they also targeted people of color, gays, the disabled, and others. Now known as the Holocaust, the extent of this atrocity, this genocide, was not discovered until the end of the war. But by 1941, the growing brutality of the Axis dictators was becoming apparent.

* * *

What was going on in Europe sounded all too familiar to Thompson and other African Americans. Blacks in America were persecuted by people who used excuses very similar to those of the Nazis: that they were "different" and "inferior."

Thompson had been more fortunate than most, but he knew what life was like for the majority of Black people. He had seen it in Wichita, his hometown, and had witnessed far more serious discrimination in his travels to live and work in other American cities. He also kept up with what was going on in Black communities in other parts of the country through the one place he could get such information: African American–owned newspapers, the Black press.[2]

Eighty percent of Black Americans lived in the southern states. Hundreds of thousands of them also read the Black newspapers. There they learned that not all states had "Jim Crow" Laws,[3] which ordered segregation, like theirs did. In the South, public places like parks, swimming pools, and restaurants had signs stating, "whites only" or "colored," which, along with "Negro," was what most African Americans were called then. Black people had to sit in the back of buses and trains and couldn't even share sidewalks with white folks. Their children had to go to separate schools, and, due to less government funding, these schools were worse than those of the white population. Too many southern Black children were deprived the education they deserved.

Black citizens in the South were also denied their right to vote. Unfair literacy tests and poll taxes, which they couldn't afford to pay, kept them from having a voice in local government to change things.

What was much worse, they suffered intimidation, threats, attacks, and even murder from some racist white people simply for being Black. Fear was no stranger to them.

In the North, there were no official Jim Crow laws, and African Americans could vote, but racial prejudice and social custom led to many of the same restrictions and disrespect for Black people. Exclusion from jobs and housing was the norm.

* * *

At the beginning of this year that had ended in war, in living rooms throughout America, people had been glued to their radios listening to President Roosevelt's State of the Union Address. It is likely that Thompson was also listening to this update on the war in Europe. And he must have been aware of the hypocrisy of some of it.

The president spoke of what he called "the Four Freedoms,"[4] which he considered essential human freedoms. The first was "Freedom of Speech and Expression"; second, "Freedom of Religion," allowing each person to worship

8

God in his or her own way; third, "Freedom from Want," which means freedom from poverty; and fourth, "Freedom from Fear."

These four freedoms may be essential, but they must be fought for and protected, often in the courts, and were not available to all Americans.

In his speech, Roosevelt also had described America's national policy as being based on "a decent respect for the rights and the dignity of all our fellow men within our gates."[5] He promised we would have the same policy toward all nations large and small.

But there was no "decent respect for the rights and the dignity" of the 13 million African Americans, 10 percent of the population, who were definitely "within our gates."

*　　*　　*

How had James G. Thompson come up with his Double V plan? Since the United States would need all the power available to defeat the enemy, he felt that "the only sensible course for the Negro and for the nation was a co-operation of equals so that democracy could be realized both at home and abroad."[6]

A cooperation of equals. A worthy goal, but how to achieve it? And now that the nation was already fighting in the war, was there time?

Thompson had read about the "V for victory" slogan popular in England where people made a "V" shape with two fingers. This gave him an idea: why not fight two wars at the same time? Have one "V" for victory overseas and another "V" for victory for African Americans, for democracy, here at home. A Double V.

It was a powerful idea, but what should he do with it?

Man making the Double V sign.
MANGOSTAR STUDIO

Thompson had previously written letters on various subjects to the editor of the *Pittsburgh Courier*, America's most popular Black-owned newspaper.[7] That might be the perfect platform for his Double V idea.

He wrote his suggestion in a letter to the newspaper's editor, P. L. Prattis.

In this letter, he stated that he strongly supported his country in this time of war and then eloquently expressed his troubled thoughts about the contradictions in the call to war. He introduced his Double V idea as a way to fight both wars at once. In mid-January 1942, James G. Thompson sent his letter on its way to the offices of the *Pittsburgh Courier*.

CHAPTER THREE

The *Pittsburgh Courier*

A Voice for the Voiceless

"We Are Americans Too! An Editorial"

The Pittsburgh Courier *calls upon all American Negros in all the parts of this vast country of ours, to support the President and the Congress that America may be victorious. We call upon the President and Congress to declare war on Japan and against racial prejudice in our country. . . . We should be strong enough to whip both of them.*
—PITTSBURGH COURIER, DECEMBER 13, 1941, I

THE EDITORS OF THE *PITTSBURGH COURIER* WERE VERY much in agreement with James G. Thompson. Five days after the bombing at Pearl Harbor and three weeks before Thompson mailed his letter to P. L. Prattis, the *Courier* had published an editorial that vowed both to support the war and to continue to deal a "knockout blow to racial prejudice within the United States." They felt that this blow must be delivered to unite all Americans in a common defense.[1]

Thompson might have read this editorial in the *Courier*, or he may have come up with the idea of two wars himself. In any case, he reinforced the notion by giving it a name and a symbol: a Double V.

* * *

Prattis and the other editors at the *Courier* were dealing with their own dilemma. For decades, the *Courier* and other Black-owned newspapers had been fighting to improve the lives of African Americans. With articles educating, inspiring, and entertaining their readers, as well as pressuring the government for changes to unfair laws and policies, they had "given voice to a people who were voiceless."[2]

Now, with the country at war, President Roosevelt and his administration were not only suggesting but also demanding that the Black press put aside its struggle against racism and focus on supporting the war.

The Black newspapers were determined to continue fighting racism *while* supporting the war. Nearly 25 years earlier, during World War I, many had agreed to the same government request to stop their push for an end to racial discrimination during the war. They had adopted a "Closed Ranks policy"[3] to "drop their grievances and pull together to make the world safe for democracy."[4] They accepted this policy because they believed that life for African Americans would be better after the war.

It wasn't.

This time, they were going to keep up their fight against racism.

When Prattis received Thompson's letter, he was intrigued.[5] This idea of a Double V, for two wars at once, might help the *Courier* and other papers in their struggle with the government.

* * *

In this digital age, we tend to forget that in the middle of the twentieth century, before television and the internet, people got their news from the radio, newspapers, and magazines. These were their eyes and ears to what was going on in their communities, the country, and the world. But most newspapers restricted their coverage to white audiences. They didn't write about the experiences that African Americans lived every day.

This gap was filled by several hundred Black-owned weekly newspapers throughout the country, publishing articles about issues and events important to African Americans. Such papers as the *Courier*, the *Chicago Defender*, and the New York *Amsterdam News* became a crucial part of life in Black communities.

A reporter at the *Chicago Defender*, Vernon Jarrett, expressed it this way: "We didn't exist in the other papers. We were [not] born, we didn't get married, we didn't die. We didn't fight in any wars, never participated in anything of a scientific achievement. We were truly invisible unless we committed a crime. And in the Black Press, the Negro press, we did get married. They showed us our babies when born. They showed us graduating. They showed our PhDs."[6]

A woman reporter at the *Courier*, Phyl Garland, described a different role of the Black press: "What weapons or what tools did Black people have in order to further their own cause or to present their argument? They were shut out of the society as a whole, but the Black press represented this sort of separate world in which Black people lived, where they could be liberated from images that were reinforced by what was taught in schools or shown in mainstream newspapers or in the movies. And it also gave them an opportunity to establish their own image, their own identity."[7]

By 1942, the *Courier* had become the most popular and widely read Black newspaper in America. Its circulation was well over 200,000 subscriptions, with a readership of close to 1 million, as each newspaper was passed around and was usually read by four or five people.[8]

Some older African Americans still remember the paper boy biking up to their homes with the *Courier* when they were kids or their parents poring over the pages spread out in the living room every Thursday. When I was telling an older Black man about my book project, he said, with tears in his eyes at the memory, that he had bought his own subscription to the *Courier* when he was 12.

Boys standing in front of the *Pittsburgh Courier* newspaper office window.
"TEENIE" HARRIS/CARNEGIE MUSEUM OF ART/GETTY IMAGES

A Pittsburgh man recalled how, when he was a child, he and his friends "used to come down the street and sit on the steps of the YMCA and look across at the *Courier* building. It had these huge glass panes, and you could see inside, and they had these big frightening machines that were constantly rolling and spinning and had these men wearing hats made of newspaper. And I always wanted to know how to make a hat out of newspaper."[9] Eventually, when he was old enough, he became a newspaper boy selling the *Courier*. And he got to wear a newspaper hat that he made himself.

* * *

Those "scary machines" (and earlier models) had been printing the *Courier* newspapers every week since 1907. In 1910, Robert L. Vann, who had been working for the *Courier* as publisher and editor, bought the paper from the previous owner.

Vann came from a very poor background, had struggled to educate himself, and became the first Black graduate of Pittsburgh Law School. In his new role at the *Courier*, he quickly became aware of the importance of politics and of how politics and communication fit together.[10] He hired outstanding writers who could bring to life his vision for this newspaper: to empower Blacks both economically and politically.

In the words of Frank Bolden, whom Vann sent to Europe to be the first Black journalist to report on the war from overseas, "There [were] only two ways to do things for him and the right way was always Vann's way. He was a hard man to reason with, but Bob Vann was a visionary. He could see around the corners."[11]

One corner that Vann saw around was how to finance his newspaper. The big advertisers—major manufacturers, large department stores, and supermarkets—wouldn't advertise in Black papers. Vann realized that without big advertising revenue, he would have to rely on selling as many newspapers as possible to keep the paper going. So the *Courier* began to publish nationally as well as locally. At its height, there were as many as 14 editions circulated in states including Texas, Louisiana, Pennsylvania, Ohio, and New York.[12] Each had the same national news and articles but also a section covering local news and events tailored to each community.

The upside of not having large advertisers was that the *Courier* and the other Black papers had the freedom to write what they wanted without fear of losing ad revenue. And the smaller ads they did get supported local Black-owned businesses. Ads for photographers, property rentals, job listings, and beauty shops informed readers of safe places for African Americans to shop and conduct business.

Besides enabling it to stay afloat, wide circulation gave the *Courier* and Robert Vann genuine political clout. It was read by all sharp politicians, especially those running for office in a district with a Black community.[13] A number of the twentieth century's most well known and influential Black journalists and intellectuals contributed articles, columns, and editorials to the *Courier*. The Black press also trained a group of photographers who showed African Americans through a dignified lens.

Many famous African Americans came through the *Courier* offices in Pittsburgh. They regularly had visits from intellectuals like scholar and activist W. E. B. DuBois; Harlem Renaissance poet Langston Hughes; A. Philip Randolph, president of the Brotherhood of Sleeping Car

Porters; Thurgood Marshall, a lawyer who was later on the U.S. Supreme Court; and Mary McCloud Bethune, who worked as an adviser for the Roosevelt administration.[14]

The editorial staff got to have lunch or get their picture taken with entertainers, such as Duke Ellington, Lena Horne, Nat King Cole, and Ella Fitzgerald, as well as with sports stars, such as Joe Lewis, Jackie Robinson, and Jesse Owens. One editor said, "You got so used to it, eventually you didn't even look up when someone famous would walk in."[15]

In return for Black newspapers showing the full spectrum of life in Black communities, African American readers treated their newspaper men and women like celebrities. "Being an entertainer or an athlete was about the only thing more glamorous than being a member of the Black press, with your byline out there so people could see your picture and your name. Everyone knew them. When they walked into a club or restaurant, everyone was excited."[16]

* * *

A weekly paper, however, was not the best way to report the news. Saturday's news was not "new" by Thursday, when the *Courier* came out. But going behind a story, running a campaign fighting for something important, could last for weeks, months, or even years and stay relevant. This was how Vann decided to keep alive awareness of the injustices of segregation.

CHAPTER FOUR

The Black Press and
the Fight for Justice

"We Are Americans Too! An Editorial"

> *We are Americans, too! From 1619 to the present day we've worked to make America ours. Our sweat and our blood, our hopes and our ambitions, our successes and our failures, are intangibly wrapped up in these forty-eight states which today present a united front.... The United States of America!*
> —PITTSBURGH COURIER, DECEMBER 13, 1941, I

THE *PITTSBURGH COURIER* CREATED CAMPAIGNS TO FIGHT many injustices. There was one to convince Blacks to switch to the Democratic Party and vote for Franklin Roosevelt for president, another to end lynching, a third to improve employment opportunities, a fourth to integrate baseball, and a fifth, the most important campaign to Robert Vann, to desegregate the military.[1]

The voting campaign started during the 1932 presidential election. Since the Civil War, most Black citizens who *could* vote had voted for Republicans. Through the years, the Republican Party kept reminding these voters that their emancipator, Abraham Lincoln, had been a Republican. But both political parties had changed, and the Republicans were now supporting the needs of African Americans less and less.[2]

With unemployment hardships increasing during the Great Depression, Vann believed that the New Deal, the program that candidate Franklin Roosevelt was proposing, would help working-class people, both white and Black.[3] Vann was determined to get Roosevelt elected president.

In a speech at a huge convention for Roosevelt and in banner headlines in the *Courier*, Vann told Blacks to "turn Lincoln's picture to the wall; the debt has been paid in full."[4] This catchy headline went to coal mines and factories and to African American communities all around the country. The message not to vote Republican spread and changed the election.[5] Blacks voted overwhelmingly Democratic and still do to this day. And Franklin D. Roosevelt became president of the United States.

*   *   *

In another campaign, the *Courier's* Wendell Smith, the first Black sportswriter to get into the writer's wing of the Baseball Hall of Fame, campaigned vigorously to get Blacks into major league baseball.[6] Back in the 1930s and 1940s, while there was a Negro baseball league with great Black players, there had been no African Americans in the major leagues since the late 1800s. Smith and the *Courier* were determined to change that. Their influential role in Jackie Robinson's becoming a Brooklyn Dodger helped break the baseball color barrier in 1947.

* * *

Another important campaign focused on the deadly secret of the American South: lynching. A *Courier* columnist and reporter, Edna Chappell McKenzie, said years later, "In my lifetime people were getting lynched all across the country. . . . We could not sit still and let this continue happening. We had to report it so that everyone would know the truth. What people don't understand is that lynching dominated life for Black southerners. People could be dragged out of their homes, with no good reason, not having done anything bad, and were lynched, while white people stood around and enjoyed it."[7] So much for "freedom from fear."

The *Courier* held a spotlight on this crime of lynching for all Americans to see. The firsthand research and reporting of McKenzie, Evelyn Cunningham, and others at the *Courier* produced riveting documentation of discrimination and lynchings.

* * *

As for the armed forces campaign, after the Pearl Harbor attack, many Blacks did go to recruiting offices to sign up to join the fight. They went to the Marine Corps and were told, "We've never had Blacks and aren't interested in having any."[8] They went to the U.S. Coast Guard and heard the same thing. Same answer at the U.S. Army Air Corps, which later became the U.S. Air Force. The U.S. Navy would accept a few, but only for jobs cooking, cleaning, and serving whites, jobs referred to as "mess duty." This was the same policy that Thompson had encountered at the Cessna aircraft company in Wichita.

Enlistees found that the army would accept them but only as 10 percent of their troops to match the percentage of African Americans in the population. This meant that many were turned away because there was no place for them.

The *Courier* had been crusading for an end to segregation policies in the military since World War I. Now, with this new war, they stepped up their effort.

But the editors of the *Courier* would have to continue their push for an integrated military without Vann. On October 24, 1940, Robert L. Vann died after a long battle with cancer.[9] The newspaper was taken over by his wife, Jessie. Ira Lewis became the new executive editor, and P. L. Prattis became the editor.

Lewis and Prattis were determined to continue the campaigns that Robert Vann had initiated, however heavy the pressure was against them. They would not give in to the government's propaganda about racial harmony at home for the sake of the war effort but would speak the truth and risk attack from the U.S. government.

Then Prattis received James G. Thompson's letter (see the appendix to view the letter in its entirety):

Dear Editor,

Like all true Americans, my greatest desire at this time, this crucial point of our history, is a desire for a complete victory over the forces of evil, which threaten our existence today. . . .

Most of our leaders are suggesting that we sacrifice every other ambition to the paramount one, victory. With this I agree, but I also wonder if another victory could not be achieved at the same time.

Being an American of dark complexion and some 26 years, these questions flash through my mind: "Should I sacrifice my life to live half American?" "Will things be better for the next generation in the peace to follow?" "Would it be demanding too much to demand full citizenship rights in exchange for the sacrificing of my life?" "Is the kind of America I know worth defending?"

The "V for Victory" sign is being displayed prominently in all so-called democratic countries which are fighting for victory over aggression, slavery, and tyranny. If this V sign means that to those now engaged in this great conflict, then let colored Americans adopt the double VV for a double victory; the first V for victory over our enemies from without, the second V for victory over our enemies within. For surely those who perpetrate these ugly prejudices here are seeking to destroy our democratic form of government just as surely as the Axis forces.

In way of an answer to the . . . questions in preceding paragraphs I might say that there is no doubt that this country is worth defending; things will be different for the next generation; colored Americans will come into their own, and America will eventually become the true democracy it was designed to be.

In conclusion let me say that though these questions often permeate my mind, I love America and am willing to die for the America I know will someday become a reality.[10]

James G. Thompson.

Prattis saw the possibilities right away. The "Double V" idea would give a name and a visual symbol to the promise the *Courier* had made in its "I Am an American, Too!"

editorial. And it was a positive image rather than the negative one the government saw. It would make it patriotic to fight both wars at once. Reporter McKenzie said, "When this young fella, Thompson, came up with the idea of the Double V, Victory at Home and Victory Abroad, it fit right into all that we lived for."[11]

Prattis so liked Thompson's idea that he decided to make it into yet another campaign for the *Courier*: a Double V campaign.

CHAPTER FIVE

The First March on Washington

"Cessna Aircraft Jim Crow Hiring Policy Continues"
by Thompson, James G.

The Cessna Aircraft Company continues its policy of discrimination. No colored applicants are taken in, other than for janitorial work or cafeteria jobs. 35 cents per hour [is the] starting wage for coloreds, all whites start at 60 cents. . . .

The head of the maintenance department said that as soon as he was allowed, he would put some on at the skilled labor wage.

—CHICAGO DEFENDER (NATIONAL EDITION),
FEBRUARY 14, 1942[1]

BACK IN WICHITA, JAMES G. THOMPSON FELT GROWING resentment at having to work in the cafeteria at Cessna. He wanted to work in the office or build planes. And he wanted to be paid fairly.

By January 1942, he and 15 other African Americans working in the cafeteria had had enough. They approached management to request a five-cent-per-hour raise.[2] When the corporation denied them the increase, these 16 men walked out on strike. They refused to work there any longer for 40 cents per hour while white employees doing the same work were paid 60 cents or more.

How did the company react? Cessna immediately hired 16 white men to replace the strikers and paid them 20 cents more per hour than it had the Black workers.[3]

While on strike, Thompson publicly expressed his indignation over this disgrace in a newspaper article he wrote, published on February 14, by both the *Chicago Defender* and the *Atlanta Daily World*—two popular Black-owned newspapers. He had been moonlighting as an Associated Negro Press reporter, and although he couldn't know it at the time, this would be the beginning of a lifelong career in journalism for him.

Two weeks later, he and nine of the other African Americans ended their strike by formally resigning from the Cessna plant in protest.[4]

*   *   *

Cessna was not alone in discriminatory hiring. In early 1941, before the United States had joined the war, President Roosevelt had announced that there was a great demand for military equipment to enable the Allies to fight and win the war. He ordered factories everywhere in the country, factories that had been manufacturing everything from lipstick cases to vacuum cleaners, to switch to manufacturing planes, warships, parachutes, and ammunition for the Allied troops in Europe, hence Thompson's move to Cessna.

Since that presidential order, billions of federal dollars in contracts had been awarded to companies to help them modify their manufacturing plants and hire more workers. These factories became the defense industry. But even in the

North, 75 percent of these companies refused to hire African Americans, while 15 percent hired them only for less-skilled jobs, as Cessna did.[5]

The owners of these companies said things like, "While we are in complete sympathy with the Negro, it is against the company policy to employ them as mechanics or aircraft workers, regardless of their training."[6] Or, as the Standard Steel Company declared, "We have not had a Negro worker in twenty-five years, and we do not plan to start now."[7] Others said that their plants lacked segregated bathrooms. Still others justified the exclusion on the basis of "maintaining harmony in the all-white workplace."[8] And, when African American women applied for war-industry jobs, some employers insulted them by saying, "My wife needs a maid."[9]

Making things worse, most trade unions were segregated. Organizations such as the American Federation of Labor (AFL) and the Congress of Industrial Organizations (CIO), which push for workers' rights, would not accept Blacks into their unions much less fight for their right to equal employment. African Americans were being left out of this employment boom.

*   *   *

Black leaders looked to President Franklin D. Roosevelt to right these wrongs. But the president had his own dilemma.

He knew that the political power of African Americans had grown, as more and more Blacks moved to northern states, where there were better jobs and the opportunity to vote. And he knew that he needed their votes to be reelected. To get this support, however, he would have to make laws and policies that would improve African American lives— but there was a problem.

Many of the senators in Congress were white southerners who were racially prejudiced and did not want the social and racial divisions in their home states to change. Roosevelt needed *their* votes and support to enact any new laws, including his New Deal programs, which aimed to swiftly stabilize the economy and provide jobs and relief to those who were suffering from the Great Depression. He couldn't risk angering them by helping the Blacks, especially with a war looming.

This political situation made it harder for the Black press and organizations to achieve their goal of ending discrimination in both the military and the defense industries. During the first half of 1941, the *Pittsburgh Courier*, the NAACP, and A. Philip Randolph were in the forefront of the effort to reach that goal.

The *Courier*'s approach, as we have seen, was to use its articles, editorials, and newspaper campaigns to convince the government to integrate the military.

The NAACP (pronounced "N double A C P" and officially called the "National Association for the Advancement of Colored People") was and still is the longest-standing organization fighting for equality for African Americans. Its approach to ending injustice was through lobbying the government and legal challenges in the courts.

A. Philip Randolph was an activist and president of the Brotherhood of Sleeping Car Porters, also known as the Pullman Porters. This was the first union of African American workers in the country to sign a labor contract with a major corporation and to be accepted into the AFL, which was very important recognition.[10] Randolph's approach was to speak boldly, think creatively, and not give up the fight.

*   *   *

The *Courier*'s employment campaign included fighting for desegregation of the defense industries. The editors believed that their readers had "so flooded their Congressmen, Senators and the President with protests, that not a single official in Washington [was] unaware of the evil" of this discrimination."[11] The *Courier* had set the stage for the fight and had, in effect, "warmed up the audience."

The NAACP's executive secretary, Walter White, was determined to get a Senate investigation into the problem of discrimination in defense plants and trade unions. To that end, he had introduced a resolution in the Senate and was lining up senators to sponsor it.[12] The process was dragging on.

Randolph, for his part, was impatient with the slow pace of results from the efforts of the *Courier* and the NAACP. He found a different, more active idea at a meeting of civil rights groups that he attended in Chicago. There, a Black woman introduced a motion for a mass demonstration in Washington. "Mr. Chairman," she said, "we ought to throw 50,000 Negroes around the White House, bring them from all over the country ... and keep them there until we can get some action from the White House."[13]

This idea excited Randolph. He not only seconded the motion but also offered to make it happen. "I agree with the sister," he said. "I will be very happy to throw [in] my organization's resources and offer myself as a leader of such a movement."[14]

In a press release on January 25, 1941, he announced his plan:

> *I suggest that 10,000 Negroes march on Washington, D.C., the capital of the nation, with the slogan: "We loyal Negro American citizens demand the right to work*

*and fight for our country."... What an impressive sight
10,000 Negroes would make marching down Pennsylvania Avenue ... with banners preaching their cause for
justice, freedom, and equality.*[15]

The event would be called the March on Washington.

* * *

Randolph predicted that this massive protest march would
expose the hypocrisy of a government that claimed to support democracy but did not support it for African Americans, a hypocrisy eloquently expressed a year later in James
G. Thompson's letter to the editor of the *Courier*. By exposing
segregation and discrimination at home, the march would
undermine the image that Roosevelt wanted for America as
the defender of freedom and democracy. This march (or the
threat of it) should make the president pay attention.

After studying other social and political movements
around the world to see what had worked for them, Randolph concluded that only power could enable the adoption
and enforcement of a policy no matter how worthy the policy might be and that this power "lies in and flows from the
masses united for a definite purpose."[16]

This was a new way to promote social change for African
Americans. The emphasis on the power of the people was a
precursor of and impetus for the civil rights marches in the
1950s and 1960s.

* * *

Randolph formed a committee to plan the event, which he
envisioned as a silent, dignified march down the streets of
the nation's capital, ending in a large demonstration at the

Lincoln Memorial. This committee would be different from the other Black activist groups, like the NAACP, which were made up of middle- and upper-class African Americans along with some white members.

Randolph did include in his committee wealthier Blacks and Black leaders, but he also gathered Black workers from all backgrounds, income levels, and classes to get balanced input for their planning. And this committee was made up entirely of African Americans.[17] These differences appealed to the public and helped the rapid acceptance and popularity of this committee and its march.

To make sure that this huge project went smoothly, Randolph invited an excellent event organizer, Layle Lane, a woman who had helped him recruit members for the Brotherhood of Sleeping Car Porters in the 1920s. Randolph also included Walter White to represent the NAACP.

White was usually cautious about committing his group to projects started by a different organization. But in a letter, Randolph diplomatically persuaded him by saying that "such a program is certain to have a favorable effect upon your splendid plan to get the whole question of national defense and the Negro probed by the Senate."[18]

This flattering approach helped convince White to join, but he had one condition. He insisted that the NAACP be represented in every meeting of the committee, to participate in all the planning and policy decisions. Randolph agreed.

The March on Washington Committee's official announcement vowed to "shake up white America, arouse official Washington and gain respect for our people."[19] To Blacks in the North and South, the announcement proclaimed, "We summon you to mass action that is orderly and lawful, but aggressive and militant, for justice, equality and freedom."[20]

The date for the march was set. July 1, 1941.

* * *

The *Courier* and the other Black newspapers had reservations about the march. They didn't think it was the right approach. The *Courier* spread the word about the planned march in articles but not on the editorial page, the heart of a newspaper, until the end of May. Then they published an editorial offering mixed support for the protest, reminding readers that the *Courier* had started this campaign against defense and military discrimination. It pointed out that even though the Black press had been working toward this goal for a long time, no Black journalist had been invited to participate in the committee.

The editorial did end with positive words about the march:

> *these efforts all aid in the fight against American color discrimination in national defense. The greatest value of these efforts lies in the effect on Negroes themselves, for in the last analysis, nobody can solve the Negro's problems but the Negro. He must be interested, informed, and organized to fight intelligently for his selfish interests, or all the pleading in the world will be amiss.*[21]

* * *

In Black communities around the country, there was great enthusiasm. Randolph had privately admitted that getting 2,000 people at the march would be quite an achievement,[22] but African Americans of all classes embraced the idea of a pilgrimage to Washington. Each state would send three to five divisions of men, women, boys, and girls. Ministers from churches across the country pledged their support. Local committees registered participants. Organizers sold buttons to raise money for transportation. They spread the word through Black newspapers. They went door-to-door handing out flyers. The goal of this March on Washington drive was to raise funds to transport marchers to the nation's capital "by bus, train, private automobile and on foot."

CHAPTER SIX

Forcing the President's Hand

*"Let's March on Capitol 10,000 Strong,
Urges Leader of Porters"*

*I suggest that 10,000 Negroes march on Washington,
D.C., the capital of the nation, with the slogan: We Loyal
Negro-American Citizens Demand the Right to Work
and Fight for our Country.*
—A. PHILIP RANDOLPH, *PITTSBURGH COURIER*,
JANUARY 25, 1941, 13

MOMENTUM FOR THE MARCH GREW RAPIDLY. BY MAY, more than 10,000 marchers planned to attend from New York City alone. More than 100,000 marchers were committed from cities and towns across the nation.[1] As the movement gathered strength, the committee decided on an official goal: get President Roosevelt to issue an executive order abolishing segregation and discrimination in the military, federal agencies, and national defense contractors.[2]

They chose this strategy because the president could enact an executive order without needing approval from the southern-led congress. This, at least temporarily, would resolve his dilemma over the southern senators.

In his many columns, interviews, and speeches, Randolph began to use a style of language new to the African American struggle for civil rights. With imagery, tone, and cadence more like that of a sermon, he said such things as, "Let no Black man be afraid. We are simply fighting for our rights as American citizens. . . . This is our own native land. Let us fight to make it truly free, democratic, and just."[3] And, in an article he wrote for the *New York Amsterdam Star-News*, Randolph said, "Let the Negro masses speak. When they speak, they will speak with the tongues of angels."[4]

This moving style of speaking was reminiscent of the speeches of the abolitionists fighting slavery in the 1800s. Martin Luther King Jr. and others in the civil rights movements of the 1950s and 1960s would come to use a similar approach.

*　　*　　*

Official Washington could no longer ignore the committee and its plans. In letters sent on June 3, Randolph invited President Franklin D. Roosevelt, First Lady Eleanor Roosevelt, Secretary of War Henry L. Stimson, and Secretary of the Navy Frank Knox to speak to the Black marchers on July 1.[5]

The administration was worried enough about so many African Americans marching through Washington, fearing possible rioting. The thought of showing support for the march by being in the middle of the marchers giving speeches was too much.

As the day of the march neared, government officials grew more nervous. Now, fearing that the March on Washington Committee might actually carry out its threat to hold the march, the Roosevelt administration pressured the organizers to call it off.

As the president's wife, Eleanor Roosevelt, was well known as a strong supporter of equal rights, Roosevelt had her act on his behalf. But, as much as she wanted equality for African Americans, she worried that the march "would tend to make Negroes lose the friends they now have" in Washington.[6] Because of these concerns, Eleanor was opposed to the march.

On June 13, Eleanor met with Randolph and White at the office of New York City mayor Fiorello La Guardia, another supporter of racial equality, who agreed that the march should be canceled for the same reasons.

Randolph and White stood firm and refused to stop the march, stating that "Negroes have reached a place in their history where it is necessary for them to make up their independent judgement, even when it is at variance with the judgement of their very best white friends."[7] There was no chance of the march being called off unless there was "an unequivocal action by the President in the form of an executive order."[8]

The *Pittsburgh Courier*'s editorial page pointed out some practical barriers to pulling off such a march in a segregated city like Washington, D.C., where most hotels and restaurants were "Whites only":

> *Everybody knows that 500 Negro visitors to Washington are sufficient to more than tax the eating and housing facilities available to colored people, while 1,000 visitors would swamp them, and 50,000 would cause a riot.*[9]

The *Courier*'s editors were becoming a reality check on Randolph's committee, pointing out real potential obstacles in its path.

A. Philip Randolph, Eleanor Roosevelt, and Mayor Fiorello La Guardia.
NEW YORK PUBLIC LIBRARY

*   *   *

When the appeal from Eleanor Roosevelt and Mayor La Guardia didn't persuade Randolph to call off the march, the president realized that he had to get involved personally. He agreed to meet with White and Randolph and several of his own advisers on June 18 in Washington. Things were moving fast.

Some of the more moderate March on Washington Committee members became nervous about demanding an executive order from the president. They were afraid that it might backfire and leave them with nothing.

At the White House meeting, to appease these moderates and as a negotiating measure, Randolph and White told the president, "Our people are being turned away at factory gates. . . . We want you to do something that will enable Negro workers to get work at these [defense] plants."[10] They knew that they would have to leave until later the demand to integrate the military.

The president offered to call a few business owners and to release a statement condemning discrimination in the defense industries.[11]

Randolph said, "Mr. President, we want you to do more than that. We want something concrete, something tangible, definite, positive, and affirmative."[12]

"What do you mean?"

"Mr. President, we want you to issue an executive order making it mandatory that Negroes be permitted to work in these plants."

"Well, Phil," Roosevelt replied, "you know I can't do that. In any event, I couldn't do anything unless you called off this march of yours."

Not wanting to give up his leverage by agreeing to call off the march before the president committed to issuing an order, Randolph said, "I'm sorry, Mr. President, the march cannot be called off."[13]

To convince the president that there was growing congressional support for such an executive order, they showed him the results of a questionnaire that the National Negro Congress had sent out to representatives and senators.[14]

Seeing that Roosevelt was still unconvinced, Randolph decided to play his winning card. He revealed to the president that 100,000 African Americans had pledged to march on July 1, only 12 days from then.

This number shocked Roosevelt. He had been led to expect a much smaller turnout for the proposed march. Not believing Randolph, the president turned to White and asked him how many marchers were expected to show up. White didn't blink. He said, "100,000, Mr. President."[15]

Roosevelt knew that he was facing a public relations disaster. The nation and the world would be watching and see the hypocrisy of America's claim to being a beacon of democracy. With this in mind, the president redirected the conversation, now asking what specific items the men wanted in the executive order.

Mayor La Guardia, who was also at the meeting with the president, was tasked with working with high government officials to create the details of an executive order. The next day, La Guardia presented the president with a memorandum of what the order should look like.

Randolph was not satisfied with the first few drafts, but on June 24, La Guardia presented an acceptable draft of the executive order to Randolph, who obtained White's approval and then that of others on the March on Washington Committee.

On June 25, 1941, only six days before the date of the march, President Roosevelt signed Executive Order 8802:

> *Prohibition of Discrimination in the Defense Industry.*[16]
> *I do hereby reaffirm the policy of the United States that there shall be no discrimination in the employment of workers in defense industries and government because of race, creed, color, or national origin.*

The order went on to establish a "Committee on Fair Employment Practices," known as the FEPC, to be appointed by the president without needing Senate approval. It would be up to this committee to receive and investigate complaints of discrimination and to take appropriate steps to resolve the grievances.

Randolph kept his end of the bargain. He postponed the march.[17]

In a radio broadcast the next day, Randolph said, "We have aided in cleansing the soul of America of the poisons of hatred and thus have given added strength to the national defense effort at the time this strength is needed."[18]

He did, however, ask the local march committees to remain intact to keep tabs on the effectiveness of this order locally.

The *Courier* praised Randolph and the committee for negotiating this executive order but had another reality check: they pointed out a potential problem with the executive order, one that would be felt by James G. Thompson six months later at the Cessna plant. The order stated that

> *all contracting agencies of the Government of the United States shall include in all defense contracts* hereafter *negotiated by them a provision obligating the contractor not to discriminate against any worker . . . but, it does not affect the defense contracts already negotiated. In other words, there are billions of dollars in contracts whose holders will not be forced to abide by the President's order because it is not* retroactive.[19]

The editorial went on in glowing terms:

> *Aside from this necessary analysis for the record, there must be a feeling of elation and relief in the breast of every American Negro and of all friends of democracy over this great forward step toward true national unity. We begin to feel at last that the day when we shall gain full rights, privileges and opportunities of American citizenship is now not far distant.*

*   *   *

Some of the March on Washington Committee members were disappointed that the march had been postponed. The harshest criticism came from Bayard Rustin, youth coordinator of the New York committee, who felt betrayed.[20] Rustin accused Randolph of compromising his principles and selling out to the president.

In reply, Randolph insisted that the march had been postponed, not canceled, and could be rescheduled if necessary. He also explained that his action had been based on the fact that its "main objective," namely, the issuance of an executive order banning discrimination in the national defense industry, had been met. The committee would have been placed in an awkward position if they had given up their main goal because they didn't get everything they wanted.[21] White backed up Randolph, and Rustin had to accept the decision.

*   *   *

A. Philip Randolph saw his postponed march come to life 22 years later in 1963 when he participated in Martin Luther King's "March on Washington." At the Lincoln Memorial that day, Randolph was the first speaker.

Bayard Rustin also finally got to have his march. He was the major organizer of that 1963 march, which ended with Martin Luther King's famous "I Have a Dream" speech to the almost 250,000 people gathered there.

The 1963 March on Washington was a success. At its end, a triumphant Rustin, who had planned this incredible event in only two months, stepped up to the microphone to read the demands that the leaders of the civil rights movement would take to President John F. Kennedy.[22]

These three important fighters for equality—the NAACP, A. Philip Randolph, and the *Courier*—would come together again and again throughout the rest of the war to encourage the government to change its discriminatory policies.

They now turned their focus to desegregating the military.

CHAPTER SEVEN

Segregation in the Military

"Editorial: The Racial Front"

The U.S. Army's policy with regard to Negro Soldiers appears to be one of segregating Negroes into Negro units, generally commanded by white officers and generally policed by white military police. The Navy's policy has been even more strict: Negros could serve the Navy only in the capacity of mess attendants—cooks, waiters, etc.
—PITTSBURGH COURIER, JANUARY 31, 1942, 18

"THE JAPANESE ARE ATTACKING US!" YELLED THE VOICE over the loudspeaker. An African American mess attendant dropped the dirty laundry that he was collecting and raced up the narrow metal stairs to his battle station on the deck of the ship *West Virginia*. Fifteen-foot flames from neighboring ships surrounded him. Blasts of explosions from torpedoes and the shriek of alarms roared through the smoke.

His battle station had been destroyed. An officer ordered him to help his injured captain, so he lifted him up and carried him out of the line of fire. Then he found an abandoned antiaircraft machine gun in the chaos. He had never fired such a gun but had seen others use it. Getting into position, he fired and kept firing at the Japanese planes swarming overhead. His barrage downed four enemy planes before the flames closed in and he had to leave the area. He moved on to help other sailors get off the ship to safety before being ordered to save himself.[1]

He was one of the first heroes at Pearl Harbor on December 7, 1941.

And nobody knew his name.

When they reported his heroic activities of that day, the navy, the War Department, and newspapers throughout America referred to him as "an unnamed Negro Navy messman," which was slang for "kitchen and dining room worker."

And they all reported it. This was a big deal.

The *Chicago Defender*, the *Baltimore Afro-American*, the *Pittsburgh Courier*, and other Black newspapers tried to find the name of this hero, with no luck. *Courier* reporter Frank Bolden did discover that the navy had logs of the African American messmen on the *West Virginia* but not their names, only numbers.[2]

The *Courier* assigned editor P. L. Prattis to shuttle back and forth from Pittsburgh to Washington to find the answer. After an extensive and expensive four months of investigating and badgering the War Department, Prattis discovered his name: Doris Miller, known as "Dorie."[3]

The March 14, 1942, *Courier* headline read "Messman Hero Identified" and announced to the world that Dorie Miller was a Black American hero.[4]

The NAACP and the *Courier* made a strong case for the government to award Miller the Medal of Honor, like they gave other heroes of that infamous day: white heroes. Secre-

Dorie Miller speaking at the U.S. Navy training center, January 1943. *NAVY/NATIONAL ARCHIVES*

tary of the Navy Frank Knox, however, said that a "letter of commendation to him was sufficient recognition."[5]

President Roosevelt overruled Knox and awarded Miller the Navy Cross, making him the first African American sailor to win this highest naval honor. It was a high honor, indeed, but Dorie Miller never received the award he deserved.

Miller was assigned to another ship after the attack, still a messman. In 1943, he came back to the United States for a brief speaking tour at naval bases as the hero he was.

A new aircraft carrier, the USS *Liscome Bay*, was his next assignment.

Six months later, Dorie Miller died, along with the rest of the crew, when a torpedo from a Japanese submarine struck the *Liscome Bay*, sinking it to the bottom of the sea.[6]

*   *   *

Dorie Miller had been assigned to mess duties: cooking, serving, cleaning, and doing laundry for the white sailors simply because of the color of his skin. The navy accepted African American volunteers only as "messmen third class."

The *Courier* angrily attacked this navy policy. "Is it fair, honest, or sensible that this country with its fate in the balance should continue to bar Negroes from service except for in the mess department of the Navy, when at the first sign of danger they so dramatically show their willingness to face death in defense of the stars and stripes?"[7]

Apparently, the navy thought it was.

The army, the only other branch of the military that allowed any Blacks to enlist at all, treated them in a similarly unfair way. More African Americans could join, but the army insisted on separate Black and white units, on segregated bases, with white officers leading the Black units. This meant that there had to be duplicate barracks, mess halls, and recreation areas at each base that housed Black soldiers.

But there weren't enough army bases with double facilities to accommodate this plan. Many African Americans who wanted to fight for their country had to wait as the army built more barracks and dining rooms. This construction was quite an expense of time and money, especially for a government at war where time and money were crucial.

Because of good weather all year long, most of the army training posts were in the South, where Jim Crow laws still reigned and the Black troops were not welcome.

In addition, Black army units were given noncombat support roles no matter what their civilian expertise might be. Rarely were they trained for combat.

As one author put it, "Black soldiers were not generally asked to carry guns, but they were ordered to carry nearly everything else."[8] Facing danger, they would build airfields and roads and transport ammunition, troops, artillery, and airplanes. But they were not allowed to fight the Axis enemy, which is what they had signed up for. And they were not given credit for the heroic, important, and necessary things they did do to help win the war.

* * *

Black newspapers and the NAACP received letters from African American soldiers all over the country complaining of the racial discrimination they experienced both on and off base.[9] While being trained for these often-dangerous, labor-intensive noncombat duties, Blacks endured brutal disrespect from many of their white officers, other white soldiers, and the surrounding communities. In the South, Black trainees could not leave the bases during their days off to ride a bus to town to go to a movie or eat a meal without encountering hateful racial taunting or violence from some of the local white residents. The white military police often sided with white perpetrators rather than support the Black soldiers. This was especially difficult for those enlistees from the North who had never had to deal with such blatant Jim Crow behavior.

A group of Black soldiers at Jackson air base in Jackson, Mississippi, together wrote that the "civilian police have threatened to kill several soldiers here. [In] some parts of Mississippi, Negro soldiers are not allowed to walk in town. Lieutenant Bromberg, . . . assists civilian police in the punishment of Negro soldiers."[10]

At Camp Bowie in Texas, Black soldiers experienced similar mistreatment. The men at the Second Battalion wrote to the *Courier* that they were jeered at by white soldiers "day and night." If they tried to defend themselves from white locals in town, they were outnumbered 10 to 1.[11] They were blamed for every incident on base and off no matter who started it. And they were called the "N-"word even by the white officers.[12]

The Black troops considered the South "worse than hell itself."[13]

And it wasn't only in the South. All army bases were segregated. Neighboring communities in other parts of the country were unpredictable as to their racial policies. A Black soldier at a base in Oregon told how they had nowhere to go on their days off because the only towns near the base were all white and, even though it was in the Northwest, there were no restaurants that would serve them or movie theaters that they could enter.

On the other hand, a Black soldier from a base in Colorado was puzzled that the recreational facilities on base were segregated, while restaurants and movies in town were integrated. The Black soldiers here ended up going into town for entertainment.

In Massachusetts, a white soldier wrote that his former company commander did not tolerate racial discrimination in his camp but that the present commander had "set his Southern policy which is ruining the morale of every soldier. . . . We are all fighting together, why can't we at least have a soda or an ice cream together?"[14]

Courier editor P. L. Prattis and the NAACP's Walter White also wondered why Black and white troops were not allowed to have a soda or an ice cream together—to eat, drink, and relax together much less fight side by side. They decided to find out.

CHAPTER EIGHT

Fighting the War Department and Jim Crow

"Army Policy Unchanged—Stimson"

Despite mounting criticism from Negro organizations upon its attitude towards the now more than 600,000 Negro soldiers in the United States Army, the War Department is standing pat on its policy of Jim Crow-ism. This brought an instant rebuke from Judge William H. Hastie, formerly civilian aide to the Secretary of War, who resigned in protest against Jim-Crow practices in the Armed Forces.
—PITTSBURGH COURIER, OCTOBER 6, 1943

"THE WAR DEPARTMENT CAN ONLY HAVE ONE RULE WHICH must apply to the army as a whole . . . , it therefore became necessary to issue a Jim Crow rule which would apply to the south and north."[1]

This was the official answer from the War Department to Walter White's and P. L. Prattis's questions about the segregation policies in the military.

Why had they chosen the Jim Crow rule to be the one for everyone? Had the War Department missed an opportunity to offer a haven from racial discrimination to Blacks in the army? Each branch of the military had its own explanation.

Secretary of the Navy Knox explained the navy's policy by saying that "the country's racial quandary is insoluble in the Navy"[2] because sailors serve aboard ships with tight living quarters. He said that there could not be northern desegregated ships and southern segregated ones. So Black sailors "would continue to serve exclusively as stewards and cooks," housed in a different part of the ship from the white sailors and eating their meals separately. He claimed that racism was "not the military's problem."[3]

Dorie Miller's heroism seemed to have had no impact on the navy's policies.

Secretary of War Stimson said that segregation and racism were deeply rooted in society and that the military shouldn't change what the men are used to.

Army Chief of Staff George C. Marshall claimed that desegregation would hurt the military's efficiency and that during the war was not a time to deal with racial issues. He also stated, perpetuating a myth, that Blacks would not be good combat soldiers, although they had fought courageously and successfully in every American war from the Revolution through World War I.[4]

The *Pittsburgh Courier* and Black leaders were appalled by this reasoning. They believed that racial discrimination could be changed in the military more easily than in the rest of society. Unlike civilians, soldiers and sailors had to follow orders and thus could be commanded to make social changes.

They also felt that during the war might be the ideal time for this, as there could be a willingness to end segregation because, with the Allies fighting deadly discrimination overseas, the U.S. government would not want the world to see its own undemocratic policies.

* * *

Shortly before America entered the war, pressure from the Black leaders and Roosevelt's need for Black votes in the upcoming election led to the appointment of William H. Hastie, a highly respected Black Harvard Law School graduate and former federal judge, to be the civilian assistant to Secretary of War Stimson.[5] Now they would have an African American champion *within* the War Department to fight for the rights of Black military personnel.

Judge William H. Hastie.
NATIONAL ARCHIVES

Hastie was determined not to be simply a rubber stamp for whatever Stimson wanted as the previous assistant had been. He was concerned that he might have been hired as a token Black in the department with no power. So to make his position clear, he issued his own statement on accepting his appointment. "I have always been consistently opposed to any policy of discrimination and segregation in the Armed Forces of this country. I am assuming this post in the hope that I will be able to work toward the integration of the colored man into the army and to facilitate his placement, training, and promotion."[6]

While Stimson, Hastie, and the War Department staff examined the army's predicament of discrimination and discord on the army bases, the Black leadership and its white supporters reached out to Judge Hastie.

Roy Wilkins of the NAACP suggested to Hastie that he specifically tell Secretary Stimson that "the chief complaint against the Army . . . is that it has surrendered completely to local prejudices and has compelled its Negro soldiers to accept brutality and discriminatory treatment in and about the camps where they are stationed."[7] Something had to be done about the contentious situation, especially at the southern training bases.

The NAACP's executive secretary, Walter White, presented General Marshall with an interesting idea endorsed by several Black newspaper editors. White suggested that General Marshall create an experimental integrated division within the army. Black and white soldiers could volunteer to serve in the division. White insisted that "this was not an idle speculation on my part."[8] His proposal had support from Judge Hastie and Undersecretary of War Robert P. Patterson.

The NAACP roused more support for such an integrated division. They found that many white Americans believed that "racial segregation in the army is undemocratic and dangerous to our national morale." Several prominent white southerners vocally supported White's proposal, as reported in a *Courier* article titled "Southerners Endorse Mixed Volunteer Army Division" in its January 24, 1942, edition.[9] The article also quoted a young white New Yorker newly inducted into the U.S. Marines who asked to be transferred to such an integrated unit were it to be created, saying that the Marine Corps' policy restricting its membership to people of the white race "does not satisfy me as being a bright, shining example of the democracy for which we are allegedly fighting."[10]

Even with this backing, the War Department rejected the proposal, saying that it "would not indulge in social experimentation in time of war."[11] General Marshall believed that "the urgency of the present military situation necessitates our using tested and proved methods of procedure and using them with all haste."[12] Their fear of change at that dangerous, high-pressure moment is understandable, but they missed another opportunity to make the racial situation in the military change more smoothly and possibly more quickly.

* * *

Since this plan didn't work, Hastie suggested exploring the possibility of replacing Black troops with white troops in the South. Stimson's answer to the problems was, where feasible, to station northern Blacks in northern bases and southern Black soldiers in southern ones, as it was harder for Black enlistees from the North, who were not used to southern ways, to be stationed in the South. They were not getting close to a practical solution and not dealing with the underlying problem.

As an interim action, in September 1941, Judge Hastie urged Secretary Stimson to at least address the issue of the frequent violence between white civilians, white military police, and Black soldiers. In a memo, he declared, "It is only the sensational cases of shootings, killings and rioting which attract public attention. But day by day, the Negro soldier faces abuse and humiliation. In such a climate resentments, hatred, fears, and misunderstandings mount until they erupt in sensational violence."[13]

Two weeks later, in an attempt to address the situation, Stimson issued a public statement that expressed the War Department's sincere concern over the disturbances involving Black soldiers, white civilians, and military police. He said that the War Department not only was "concerned in achieving justice, but it was determined to correct the causes that led to the racial conflicts in order to raise the morale of all soldiers." Stimson also spoke of the military police as "respectable soldiers who should not be feared and who should maintain law and order without unnecessary force." Finally, he maintained, "Recent affrays between the colored soldiers and white civilians are also under investigation. The army will not tolerate breaches of discipline by its personnel or assault upon soldiers engaged in line of duty. Most soldiers and civilians will meet on a plane of mutual respect and understanding."[14]

This memo sounded good, but Hastie thought that it was unrealistic; if Stimson thought that such a memo would resolve the issue, he was naive. There were insufficient steps put in place by the army to achieve and enforce these policies. Nothing really changed.

Sensing that it might be easier to modify the on-base behavior of white soldiers and officers than that of outside communities, Hastie requested that Stimson focus on that.

So Simpson sent another memo addressed to the commanding generals across the world and all base commanders. It officially banned the use of racial slurs and insulting language by officers to enlisted men, of using racial epithets, such as calling Black soldiers "boy" or using the N-word.

The commanders were instructed to observe the following: "superiors are forbidden to injure those under their authority by radical or capricious conduct or by abusive language."[15] And men under their command should be treated "as to preserve their self-respect."

For the first time in U.S. military history, the army had officially banned the use of racial epithets and insulting language. This action was another signal that the army was, however reluctantly, making some noteworthy shifts in race relations. But the continued letters of complaint from Black soldiers after 1942 indicate that the directive was disregarded by many white officers.

*   *   *

By 1943, there was still little improvement in the racial situation in and around army bases. Hastie was growing more and more frustrated with what little change all his work had produced. On January 18, 1943, he resigned his post as Stimson's civilian assistant. He believed that he could get more done as an activist outside the government.

In that role, in June 1943, Hastie released a prepared statement to the *New York Daily News* that he believed explained the army's indecisiveness regarding racial issues: "Both the administration and the military authorities persist in trying to muddle through, without plan or program, hoping that somehow things will come out all right."[16] He complained that they were dealing with each incident as it occurred. Investigations and reports, an occasional court-martial, or the removal of some individual from his company were not ending the problem.

He pointed out that for the soldiers overseas, the army was "busy with booklets [and] lectures . . . teaching our soldiers how to treat the peoples of India, the South Sea islanders, the Arabs, everywhere but the fellow American soldiers. It is time that similar efforts and techniques be employed in the business of building comradeship within our own military and civilian communities."[17]

The wide publicity that Dorie Miller's heroism had received immediately after Pearl Harbor back in December 1941 had given African Americans around the country immediate and personal interest in the war. To build on this new awareness in the Black community, six weeks later, the *Courier's* editors launched its Double V campaign.

CHAPTER NINE

Rolling Out the Double V Campaign

ON JANUARY 31, 1942, TWO WEEKS AFTER THOMPSON mailed it, *Pittsburgh Courier* readers opened their newspapers to find James G. Thompson's letter to the editor in the very center of page 3. Above it was the title "Should I Sacrifice to Live 'Half-American?'"[1]

Just the letter and a photo of Thompson with this brief introduction appeared below the title:

> *Editor's Note: A young man, confused and befuddled by all of this double talk about democracy and the defense of our way of life, is asking, like other young Negroes, some very pertinent questions. We reprint this letter in full because it is symbolic.*[2]

The next week's paper had an unusual drawing in the upper left corner of the front page. One of the *Courier's* cartoonists had designed a logo to represent the Double V campaign: two Vs with the words "Double Victory" and "Democracy at Home and Abroad." A small version of this emblem appeared at the bottom of pages 5, 7, and 13.

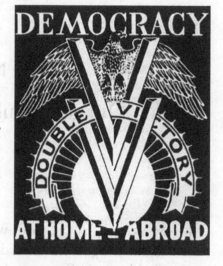

Double V logo.
PITTSBURGH COURIER ARCHIVES/
NEW PITTSBURGH COURIER

Just the drawings. No explanation.[3]

On February 14, the following week, a banner appeared across the top of page 1.[4]

The banner explained that the previous week, "without any public announcement or fanfare," the editors of the *Courier* had introduced their emblem with the war slogan "a double 'V' for a double victory" to see how their readers would respond. Overwhelmingly, hundreds of telegrams and letters of congratulations poured in. The Double V campaign's rollout had begun.

The *Courier's* Double 'V' for a Double Victory Campaign Gets Country-wide Support

 Last week, without any public announcement or fanfare, the editors of The Courier introduced its war slogan- a double "V" for a double victory to colored America. We did this because we wanted to test the response and popularity of such a slogan with our readers. The response has been overwhelming. Our office has been inundated with hundreds of telegrams and letters of congratulations, proving that without any explanation, this slogan represents the true battle cry of colored America. ...

PITTSBURGH COURIER ARCHIVES/NEW PITTSBURGH COURIER

One of the letters printed in this issue was from James G. Thompson himself, thanking the *Courier* for printing his letter. It said,

> *Dear Editor:*
>
> *I wish to compliment the staff of the* Pittsburgh Courier *and especially William G. Nunn, the artist who drew the sketches for the "Double V" for Victory signs appearing in the* Courier *last week. It is my fond hope that these may lead to the eventual elimination of discrimination and prejudices. If they should pave the way for this, my efforts in this direction will be amply rewarded.*
>
> *My idea in presenting this to the* Courier *was the hope that it would take on the proportions of a nationwide drive in which every home and every car would carry in full view these Double "V" for victory signs.*[5]
>
> *James. G. Thompson*

The *Courier*'s readers had the same idea of spreading the word with Double Victory signs. They suggested that the *Courier* make Double V pins, badges, posters, and bumper stickers: a good plan that the *Courier* acted on.

From that day forward, each issue of the *Courier* had more mentions of the Double V than the last: articles, photos, letters to the editor, and endorsements from famous people. Everywhere the readers looked, they were reminded of the Double V campaign.

Enthusiastic African American readers soon formed Double V clubs around the country, sponsoring activities such as Double V dances, Double V beauty contests, and Double V baseball games. Double V gardens were planted. Women sewed Double Vs onto their clothing and invented a new Double V hairstyle.[6]

The *Courier* encouraged these clubs and began a "Double V Club News" column in each weekly issue. Five cents bought a Double V pin, and stickers cost a penny apiece. All the proceeds would be donated to help America win the war.

In May, there were 38 Double V clubs in all. Three months later, the number had grown to 206 clubs in 34 states with a total of 200,000 members.[7]

The Double V clubs were not only for fun. The campaign gave club members a framework for acting against racial discrimination. Some wrote to congressmen to protest the voting poll tax, and others demonstrated in front of department stores telling Black patrons not to shop at stores that refused to hire them or barred them from using the dressing rooms. Still others met with business officials to promote nondiscriminatory hiring.

The biggest club activity, however, was supporting the war effort. Club members gathered rubber and tin for the defense industries. They collected clothing, books, candy, and cookies to send to Black enlistees reporting for duty. Along with generating tens of thousands of dollars for the war effort from the purchase of pins and posters, the clubs sold millions of dollars' worth of war bonds.[8] Soon, club members' children joined in the excitement. They helped gather materials and learned about their parents' antidiscrimination activities. These children would be adults in the 1950s and 1960s ready to participate in the civil rights movement.

Throughout the spring, other Black newspapers joined the Double V campaign, publishing the symbol, photos, and Double V articles. They began to support the Double V partly because it was so popular and they didn't want to lose market share to the *Courier* but also, and more important, because the editors realized the impact that America's losing the war could have on African Americans. The press saw the Double V as a way to raise low Black morale so that they would join the fight. America needed all the fighting strength available to help the Allies win the war.

The NAACP's Walter White reminded members that, as bad as things were in the United States, they would be worse if Hitler won the war. Edgar T. Rouzeau, editor and manager of the *Courier*'s New York office, wrote, "If the United States is a loser in World War II, then Black America may not emerge victorious in its war at home. Although we have not enjoyed our full share of democracy in 'democratic America,' our chances of enjoying any democracy at all in a totalitarian America would be far more doubtful."[9]

Columnist George Schuyler compared the bombing of Pearl Harbor to horrific lynching incidents, including an especially brutal one in Sikeston, Missouri. In both the bombing and the lynchings, he wrote, innocent young men were attacked without warning. He went on, "The 'Double V' campaign ... takes on added meaning when we consider incidents like these. One victory goes along with the other. Negroes would be more enthusiastic about obtaining victory abroad if America would stop lynching young Negroes at home."[10]

A powerful letter to the editor about the Sikeston lynching, written by James G. Thompson, appeared in the same issue of the *Courier*. He called the Sikeston mob "traitors to the cause of democracy. They seek to destroy the foundations of our government as Hitler and company. These things are no longer a threat to a minority of Americans; but a direct threat to all Americans."[11]

On a lighter note, the Double V campaign inspired some prominent people and organizations. Walter White and his NAACP were strong advocates. The CIO and other unions supported it. A. Philip Randolph applauded the increased public enthusiasm for fighting segregation at home.

Support also came from famous white people. Politicians such as Wendell Willkie, who ran for president against Roosevelt in 1940, wore Double V pins on their lapels. Hollywood came out for the Double V too, with big movie stars such as Humphrey Bogart, Ingrid Bergman, and Gary Cooper strongly in favor.[12]

The music industry was a big Double V campaign supporter. A song called "Yankee Doodle Tan" became a hit with the popular big bands of the time. Thousands of people danced to Double V songs as Black bandleaders Lionel Hampton and others performed at clubs and theaters and played to millions of listeners on the radio.

The Ink Spots, one of the first Black singing groups popular with both Black and white audiences, with 30 hits on the pop charts, appeared in a photo in the *Courier* performing "Yankee Doodle Tan." And who should be in the back row of the group singing along but James G. Thompson.[13]

Thompson was surprised by a visit from bandleader Jimmie Lunceford, who flew his small private plane to Wichita, Kansas, to play at a big dance there. Lunceford came onstage displaying the Double V insignia and praised "Wichita's own James Thompson" for starting the Double V. The next day, Lunceford gave Thompson a ride in his plane, Thompson's first flight ever.[14]

It was two weeks later that editor P. L. Prattis sent George S. Schuyler to interview Thompson in Wichita. On his return, Schuyler described Thompson as "the idol of Wichita's 6,000 Negro citizens." He also reported to the editors that Thompson was a government civil service worker and a freelance reporter, not only the cafeteria worker they thought he was.[15]

James G. Thompson (in back) singing with the Ink Spots about the Double V.
"TEENIE" HARRIS/CARNEGIE MUSEUM OF ART/GETTY IMAGES

When Schuyler shared the news that Thompson had quit his job at the Cessna cafeteria after being refused a five-cent-per-hour raise, the editors knew how they could get Thompson more involved in the campaign. They offered him the job of managing the nationwide Double V campaign and even agreed to pay for his move to Pittsburgh.[16] Thompson was not about to pass up this opportunity.

As the new director of the *Courier's* national Double V campaign, Thompson arranged events and marketing and wrote articles for the *Courier*. Thompson was now a real, full-time journalist.

The focus of the Double V clubs on supporting the war was crucial to Prattis and the other editors of the *Courier*. The federal government, especially FBI director J. Edgar Hoover, continued to pressure them to stop printing pro-Black-rights articles during the war and to only back the war effort. The Double V campaign proved they could do both: patriotically support the war and continue to push for equal rights for African Americans. Prattis and his colleagues hoped this would be enough.

CHAPTER TEN

"Stop the Black Presses!"

"Is Criticism to Be Suppressed?"

We were criticizing these flaws in the structure of Democracy in this country long before any of the Axis dictators came to power, and we continue to criticize them because they injure our COUNTRY. If such . . . is regarded as "fostering disunity," then the real blame must be borne by those who insist on maintaining the color bar, and not by the Negro press.
> —*PITTSBURGH COURIER* (CITY EDITION),
> MAY 16, 1942, 6

THE *PITTSBURGH COURIER*'S EDITORS MIGHT HAVE BELIEVED that their Double V campaign, for "Victory Abroad and Victory at Home," was patriotic, but the president in 1942 didn't think it was patriotic at all.

To President Roosevelt, the Double V campaign was a promise that the Black press would continue to criticize the government and military even though the country was at war. He had fully expected them to stop all criticism as most of them had done during World War I.

The press, obviously, didn't plan to do that this time.

Security was high on the list of the government's priorities. Danger lurked not only overseas but also in the United States, at least in the minds of some government officials. They believed that continuous surveillance was necessary to locate possible spies, traitors, or anyone undermining the public's support of the war.

Leaking military information, encouraging disloyalty, supporting the enemy, or criticizing the government was considered "sedition." President Roosevelt wanted all sedition suppressed during the war.[1]

He was joined in this concern by four other departments of the federal government: the FBI, the Justice Department, the Post Office, and the military.

The president's right-hand man in this effort was FBI director J. Edgar Hoover. The powerful Hoover was even more determined than Roosevelt to uncover and stop possible sabotage. He relentlessly investigated what he considered enemy communities in the United States, sharing his findings in a monthly report to the president.

Hoover kept an eye on the activities and publications of Germans, Japanese, and Italians in America, people who themselves or whose parents had come from the enemy countries and, he thought, might be tempted to support their homelands. He searched for fascist groups who agreed with Hitler's beliefs and actions and for communists.[2]

And both he and President Roosevelt were watching the Black press.

They worried that the Black newspapers' criticism of the military would hurt morale and discourage Black enlistment. They weren't sure America could win the war without 10 percent of its fighting force if African Americans didn't enlist.

J. Edgar Hoover, director of the FBI.
HARRIS AND EWING, LIBRARY OF CONGRESS

They also feared that this criticism would undermine the discipline and compliance of African Americans who *did* enlist in the army and navy.

And they were concerned about how the United States would look to other countries. C*ourier* reporter Edna Chappell

McKenzie believed that "they wanted to shut us down because we were doing something which held the United States of American government up to the ridicule of the whole world. How can you go somewhere and fight for democracy when you have people that you are oppressing by law?"[3]

The *Courier* found this sudden concern for Black morale "astonishing, amusing, and shameful." In an editorial on May 2, 1942, it printed the following:

> *It is* astonishing *to find supposedly informed persons in high positions so unfamiliar with the thought and feeling of ⅒ of the population. One would imagine they had been living on another planet.*
>
> *It is* amusing *to see these people so panicky over a situation which they have caused, and which governmental policies maintain.*
>
> *It is* shameful *that the only remedy they are now able to put forward is Jim Crowism on a larger scale and suppression of the Negro newspaper.*

It concluded, "Squelching the Negro newspapers . . . will only further depress the morale."[4]

*   *   *

The president and the FBI were powerful, but, like police, they could only investigate and make arrests. Convictions and sentencing in each case depended on the Justice Department led by Attorney General Francis B. Biddle.[5]

Fortunately for the Black press and the country, Attorney General Biddle was a strong believer in constitutional rights, especially freedom of speech and freedom of the press, even during wartime.[6]

Biddle became the central player in the fight against the suppression of the Black press.

The Post Office was involved because it was responsible for mailing newspapers and magazines to readers around the country. President Roosevelt pressured Postmaster General Frank Walker to make sure that no seditious statements were sent through the mail. So Walker ordered thousands of publications to be sent to his department so that they could determine if they were seditious and therefore unmailable. If they could hold one issue from being mailed on schedule, they could revoke the publisher's second-class mail status, which offered lower postal rates. Paying full mailing costs would likely bankrupt many publishers.

But the Post Office too could only recommend that a publication be stopped. It was up to the Justice Department and Attorney General Biddle to determine if something was mailable. As much as they tried, the Post Office didn't succeed in stopping the newspapers, but the threat was always hanging over the Black press.

* * *

Like President Roosevelt and Hoover, the military felt threatened by the Black press's criticism, especially of the army. The papers were broadcasting the segregation on military bases and the problems Black soldiers faced especially (but not only) in the South. Military leaders worried that this made the country look bad as well as undermining military discipline.

Because of freedom of the press, the Justice Department would not allow the War Department to order the Black newspapers to stop printing or to officially ban them from army bases. So to block the soldiers from reading them, the army gathered any Black newspapers that arrived for soldiers and hid or destroyed them. They made sure no copies of such papers were available in the base libraries or common areas. They even confiscated Black papers from newsboys and burned the papers to keep them out of the hands of the many Black soldiers who looked forward to the weekly *Courier*.[7]

Timuel Black, a teenage draftee, voiced what many Black soldiers felt about the Black newspapers. He said, "The Army, for me, was a very bad experience. Hated every minute of it, but it was uplifting when the Black papers would come through. It was a morale booster because usually the papers told what Black soldiers were doing."[8] Another soldier said, "We read The *Courier* and . . . it was a friend who . . . let us know that they were looking out for our interests."[9]

* * *

Hoover, the Post Office, and the Defense Department sent many cases they considered seditious to the attorney general. Biddle's decision was usually that the accused people or publications were only voicing opinions, not threatening the security of the country. He was not going to let anyone jeopardize the freedoms of speech and press.[10] All his investigators followed his lead and found very few cases of sedition.

Frustrated by the reaction of the Justice Department to his cases, Hoover sent agents to Black newspaper offices. FBI agents sat outside the offices of the *Courier* and other Black papers monitoring everyone who came and went. But as *Courier* reporter Frank Bolden recalled years later, "The agents never [seriously] harassed anybody or threatened anybody. They just expressed their dissatisfaction at what we were doing."[11] So the Black editors were not worried.

Francis Biddle, attorney general.
LIBRARY OF CONGRESS

What did unnerve them, though, was the FBI subscribing to every Black newspaper in the country. The FBI wanted them to know that nothing in the newspapers would get by them.

* * *

Meanwhile, Roosevelt was pressuring Attorney General Biddle to take legal action against newspapers for sedition. Biddle had more serious issues on his plate than the Black press, which he didn't believe was seditious. But the president was relentless.

Fortunately, Biddle had a politically astute assistant, James H. Rowe Jr.,[12] who suggested that the department could improve its image immediately and reassure the president by moving quickly and publicly against some of the extreme radical seditionists: the fascist and communist publications. This would take the pressure off the Black press.

Biddle wasted little time in following Rowe's suggestion. The vigilant Hoover had gathered more than enough information on radicals for the attorney general to move immediately.

When some of these radical publications were taken to court, though, the Black editors became nervous. Rumors flew that the Black papers were about to be shut down. The publishers increased the number of letters, articles, and editorials they sent to government officials showing that they did, in fact, support the war.

*   *   *

P. L. Prattis from the *Courier* and John L. Sengstacke, publisher of the *Chicago Defender*, tried to meet with officials in person in Washington, D.C., but found it difficult to get appointments. Sengstacke finally asked Mary McLeod Bethune of the president's Black cabinet to arrange a meeting for him with Biddle, which she managed to do.

As Sengstacke entered the room for the meeting, Biddle was there to meet him. Spread out on a table were Black newspapers. Biddle said, "See these newspapers? These are hurting the war effort and if you don't stop writing this stuff, we're going to take some Black publishers to court under the Espionage Act."[13]

If Biddle was trying to intimidate Sengstacke, it didn't work. Sengstacke responded, "What are we supposed to do about it? These are facts and we aren't going to stop." He argued that the Black press, in urging African Americans to support the war, was obligated to express its readers' outrage

John Sengstacke (right), general manager, *Chicago Defender*.
LIBRARY OF CONGRESS

when their military contributions were wasted or rejected. Rather than instilling Black dissatisfaction, Sengstacke pointed out, it was merely reporting it.

He also had the nerve to say that Biddle must not have read any Black newspapers before the war, as they had been disclosing the horrors of racial discrimination in the military and elsewhere for decades. And their mission was as relevant as ever.

Then Sengstacke decided to call Biddle's bluff. "You have the power to close us down," he said, staring firmly into the attorney general's eyes. "So, if you want to close us, go ahead and attempt it."

Biddle was stunned into silence.

Sengstacke pressed on. "I've been trying to get an appointment to see U.S. War Secretary Stimson. I've been trying to get in touch with everybody else. Nobody will talk to us. What do you expect us to publish? We don't want to publish the wrong information. We want to cooperate with the war effort. But if we can't get the information from the heads of the various agencies, we have to do the best we can." Biddle was surprised. He had not been aware of this issue. His tone changed immediately.

"Let me see if I can help you in that way," he said, and he picked up the phone, called Secretary of the Navy John Knox, and made an appointment for Sengstacke to see him. By the end of Biddle's conversation with Sengstacke an hour later, the attorney general had promised that as long as the Black press did not publish anything more critical than what had already appeared, it would be left alone.[14] Sengstacke quickly spread the word to other Black publishers that there would be no sedition indictments.

After the successful meetings with Biddle and then Knox, the Black press did gain access to government officials, though they still could not attend the White House press conferences. Things were beginning to improve.

But in the South, army bases were still blocking Black newspapers, and the *Courier* had stopped arriving to its Black readers. There was still more to do.

Chapter Eleven

Journalism's "Underground Railroad"

THE *PITTSBURGH COURIER* HAD A NEW DILEMMA TO SOLVE. Letters flooded in from readers living in the South and from soldiers stationed there, wondering why their newspapers had stopped arriving. The *Courier* was sending papers to these southern customers every week, so where were they going? Maybe A. Philip Randolph's network of Pullman porters, already in place on trains throughout those states and already acting as a "journalistic underground railroad," could help the *Courier* find out.

But who were the Pullman porters? And how were they a "journalistic underground railroad"?

Pullman train cars were luxurious sleeper cars added to most passenger trains for their wealthy and middle-class customers. They looked like fancy hotels inside and served the best food and offered the finest towels, sheets, and service. Since the mid-1800s, George Pullman's company had been hiring only African American men as porters to treat the travelers in an elegant style.[1]

Pullman porters ranged from illiterate Black men, who often learned to read from the newspapers left on trains and their coworkers, to college students earning money to

Brotherhood of Sleeping Car Porters logo.

ILLUSTRATION FROM 1934, WHEN THE BROTHERHOOD OF SLEEPING CAR PORTERS WAS ACCEPTED INTO THE AMERICAN FEDERATION OF LABOR

pay for books and tuition. Some even became porters after getting law or medical degrees to earn enough money to open their own offices. Many famous men were either porters themselves or the sons of porters, such as Chief Justice Thurgood Marshall, the NAACP's Roy Wilkins, civil rights activist Malcolm X, and the *Courier*'s own Robert Vann.[2]

In their crisp blue uniforms, these porters helped arriving passengers with their luggage and onto the train. They changed the seats to beds while the people were at dinner and back to seats during breakfast. They delivered with a smile tea, blankets, or whatever else a rider wanted and spent most nights shining expensive shoes while the travelers slept. They even sometimes took care of the children on the train.

But that wasn't all these porters did. They also secretly gathered news stories for the *Courier*. Pullman porters were *re*porters too.[3]

The white travelers trusted the porters with their valuables and even their children while on the train but certainly

Pullman porter making up an upper berth aboard the "Capitol Limited."
LIBRARY OF CONGRESS

wouldn't off the train.[4] Many didn't even call the porters by their names, although they could see the porter's name badges. They called them all "George."[5]

To the passengers, they were anonymous, pleasant servants who quietly went about their business, ignoring any taunts, rudeness, or bullying they got from some of the riders. The porters needed their jobs and the tips that supplemented their meager salaries and so couldn't react the way they really wanted to.

Little did the travelers know that the porters were listening carefully to their conversations. They overheard those of politicians, businessmen, and even movie stars on the train who spoke openly in front of these "invisible" servants. Porters sometimes heard breaking news that would interest the *Courier*'s editors. They gathered up scattered newspapers and magazines from all over the country that passengers left behind and carried them back to Pittsburgh after reading them themselves. The stories the porters delivered would often be information the editors would not have heard about otherwise. And the *Courier* would print some in the next issue.[6]

*   *   *

Trains were the most common method of travel, at that time, to the next town or the next state, as train travel was affordable, available, and convenient—not so convenient for African Americans in the South, however.

There, Blacks travelers had to ride in separate train cars at the back of the train. They were barred from eating in diners at the train stations and couldn't even use the bathrooms there. They learned to plan carefully and bring their own food. When trains entered the South from the North, they even had to leave the cars they were riding in and go to another car at the back of the train.

The Pullman porters were the only African Americans who could travel easily in and out of the South—while they were working, at least. They also couldn't eat at the train stations. So they went to the nearest Black part of town for meals and overnight layovers between shifts.

In these Black neighborhoods, it was the porters' turn to be treated like royalty. To many other African Americans, Pullman porters seemed to have made it. They looked important in their uniforms and, with the knowledge, speech, and behavior they had picked up on the Pullman cars, had an air of sophistication.[7] And they had traveled all over the country.

Porters would introduce the locals to the *Courier* (if they didn't already know about it), get more subscriptions to the paper, and deliver by hand bundles of newspapers to be sold. They shared the latest news they had picked up in their travels. In return, the locals would update them on the latest gossip and news—more stories for the *Courier*'s editors. The

Pullman porter in train.
NEW YORK PUBLIC LIBRARY

Pullman porters brought the news and views of the working-class African Americans to the newspaper.

The porters became suspicious when they stopped finding *Courier* newspapers at the train stations for them to take to town. Some scouted around to see what was going on. They discovered men with badges on their shirts sneaking stacks of newspapers from the train. Then they tossed them into flaming metal barrels. The white sheriffs, deputies, and others were destroying the *Couriers* before they could be delivered to readers.[8]

This news from the porters explained the customers' letters. Now the editors had to find a way to stop this destruction and get the newspapers to their southern readers and soldiers on the army bases. But how?

They couldn't really look to the federal government to assist them with all the tension between them. If they sent reporters, either Black or white, to the train stations to reason with the sheriffs, they would likely be arrested or harmed.

The porters were a logical group to fix the situation because they went to every train station and were more or less ignored there. But if the porters interfered, they too would probably be arrested or beaten. And while some porters had stops on their routes near army bases, they couldn't enter the bases and had no way to save the newspapers from destruction there even if they could.

The *Courier* would have to find a way to avoid using the actual train stations as delivery pickup points in the South. And they would have to figure out how to get the papers to Black soldiers outside the base.

* * *

The editors remembered a plan that the *Chicago Defender* had put in place decades earlier. They decided to try a similar operation. The Pullman porters would *smuggle* the *Couriers* into the South![9]

They took their idea to A. Philip Randolph, who arranged it with the porters. It would be complicated and risky, but it just might work. They called their plan "Stop and Drop."[10]

Late at night, a *Courier* truck, disguised so that nobody would notice it being there at such an unusual hour, would pull up to a waiting train at the Pittsburgh station. Men would silently unload bundles of newspapers wrapped in waterproof paper. With the Pullman porters' help, they would hide these bundles in lockers in the Pullman car, in corners, under mattresses, and even beneath the train cars.[11]

Then the train would head off into the night.

A few miles before Chattanooga, Tennessee; Montgomery, Alabama; or other southern towns and cities, the porters would toss bundles of newspapers from the moving train at a prearranged location. Preachers and others from the nearby Black community would be there waiting for the newspapers.[12]

But could the porters be sure that the locals *would* be there? And, if so, would they be able to hide the bundles in their cars to take them back to the churches, barbershops, and newsstands in town?

The porters would double-check their map as the train approached the designated place. Their view would be hampered by the dark at nighttime and the speed of the train at any time. The rumble of the train would drown out any other sound. They would have to trust their map and careful coordination with the Black communities.

But what would happen if they weren't there and *Courier* newspapers were found all over the ground? Would the plan be discovered? Would the porters be arrested? They hoped they'd never find out.

Usually, the people were there, waiting. They hid all the newspapers in case they were stopped on their way back to town. And they successfully got the papers to their community.

Despite all the potential problems, with a few tweaks to the plan now and then, "Stop and Drop" worked. And it worked for years.

Now for the soldiers. For the army bases, the arrangement was to get the newspapers, in the same way, to the few Black clubs, bars, and restaurants in the towns around the base where soldiers would go during their time off.[13] There the men could read their *Couriers* every week without the officers knowing. Problem solved.

The Pullman porters did this newspaper delivery week after week throughout the war, smuggling 100,000 newspapers per week. Sometimes there were mishaps, but for the most part, their plan worked smoothly. When gradual changes to segregation in the South eased the risk and the newspapers were no longer in danger, this delivery service tapered off until it wasn't necessary.

* * *

Quite an amazing and fascinating group were the Pullman porters. And they weren't the only ones helping African Americans and the war effort behind the scenes. Many Black women were too.

CHAPTER TWELVE

African American Women Fight for Victory at Home and Abroad

"Bethune Re-Pledges Loyalty of Women"

On behalf of the womanhood of the Country and particularly Negro Womanhood, we hereby pledge ourselves . . . to the service of America defending its freedom and integrity. We voice again at this point that, "it must be all out, or it is all over."
—MARY MCLEOD BETHUNE, PRESIDENT, NATIONAL COUNCIL OF NEGRO WOMEN, INC., *PITTSBURGH COURIER*, DECEMBER 13, 1941, 10

IT WAS THE FIRST DAY OF TRAINING FOR THE NEW WOMEN'S Army Corps (WAC) at Fort Des Moines, Iowa, in 1942. The African American women officer candidates filed into the mess hall for dinner. There they discovered, squeezed into a back corner of the large hall, a table with a sign reading "Colored." After a long day of training just as hard as the white candidates, they would have to sit separately for meals. Angry but hungry, they sat at the table and ate their dinner.[1]

That evening, they came up with a plan. They couldn't change the fact that they had to live in segregated barracks while training, but this "Colored table" rule might be one they could impact.

The next night, at the same table, rather than getting in line to get their food, they turned over their plates and ate no dinner. The following evening, the "Colored" sign was gone, but in its place was a smaller one saying "For C." Again, they turned over their plates and didn't eat.

After a few more days of this behavior, they entered the mess hall, and the sign was gone.[2] So they sat wherever they wanted and enjoyed their dinner.

These Black women found a firm, quiet way to change one policy in one mess hall. Multiply that by the many other such women working actively and nonviolently during the war to end discrimination, and you have a preview of the fight a decade later to integrate schools, lunch counters, bus seats, and more.

Black women faced a double hurdle. They had to overcome discrimination against African Americans as well as that against women. Brave Black women fought these boundaries on the home front and in the military to help win a double victory.

The fact that there were African American women in the WAC at all was due largely to Mary McLeod Bethune. She had been part of the Roosevelt administration and was, at that stage of the war, working in the War Department.[3]

In 1942, women weren't allowed to enlist in the military and certainly not for combat. That May, because of a growing need, Congress approved the WAC doing such jobs as office clerk, cook, truck driver, and messenger to free up more men to fight the enemy.[4]

Mary McLeod Bethune.
NEW YORK PUBLIC LIBRARY

But the new women's corps was to be white women only. Bethune worked hard to change this rule. She even enlisted her close friend Eleanor Roosevelt to speak to her husband to help. Together, they persuaded government and army officials to include African American women in the WAC and even to train Black officers.

* * *

It wasn't just in the military that jobs usually done by men needed filling. When people think of American women during World War II, they often picture "Rosie the Riveter," the nickname for the women, with their hair tucked beneath red and white polka-dot scarves, working in defense plants while the men were overseas. These women took over welding and riveting jobs, building jeeps, ships, parachutes, and other equipment needed for the war.

Posters from that time show white and Black women working together at these jobs, but Black women were the last to be hired by these factories and then, as James G. Thompson had found at Cessna Aircraft, only for kitchen and janitorial work.[5]

Eventually, the need for workers became so great that the defense plants realized that they had to train Black women to work at the skilled jobs too. These Black "Rosies" still faced some discrimination from their coworkers and supervisors, but they acquired important new skills and added to the war effort.

*   *   *

Many Black women who were not in the military or the factories became activists and organizers in the fight to eliminate racial discrimination in America.

A. Philip Randolph's March on Washington in 1941, for example, began with an idea voiced by a Black woman at a conference. Randolph brought in another woman, Layle Lane,[6] to organize the march. She formed and led the committee that planned the entire buildup of 100,000 Black citizens committed to marching on Washington, D.C. So important was her role in the project that she attended Randolph's and White's meeting with President Roosevelt: the meeting that ended with Executive Order 8022 to desegregate the defense industry and with the postponement of the march. During that meeting, Lane told the president that Black citizens needed to "make life uncomfortable for all those who have to be reminded of the meaning of our fundamental principles."[7]

Layle Lane.
NEW YORK PUBLIC LIBRARY

Although the march did not happen, Lane and her committee continued to fight against discrimination. They called their organization the March on Washington Movement (MOWM).

E. Pauline Myers managed the MOWM central office and oversaw local chapters around the country.[8] To raise money for the organization, Myers wrote pamphlets that the members could sell. One was called "Non-Violent, Good Will, Direct Action," describing a new tactic for fighting discrimination.[9]

Myers spread the word about this new strategy in speeches to groups around the country, explaining, "The need is for mass organization with an action program— aggressive, bold, and challenging in spirit, but nonviolent in character. It invites attack, meeting it with a stubborn and

89

nonviolent resistance that seeks to recondition the mind and weaken the will of the oppressor."[10]

It was a turning point in the fight against discrimination.

Part of this new direction was to hold huge rallies in major cities, arranged by activist women from the MOWM and other Black women's organizations. Speakers, music, and other activities would inspire the thousands of mostly Black attendees to fight for "Victory at Home" in this new way.

An article in the June 27, 1942, *Courier* announced such a rally in Chicago: "A protest mass meeting . . . sponsored by the March-on-Washington Committee, is expected to bring 20,000 Negroes to the Coliseum on Friday night with A. Philip Randolph, Walter White, and Dr. Mary McLeod Bethune listed as principal speakers."[11]

There were at least 25,000 people at the actual event, filling the Coliseum and spilling out into the street, where speakers broadcast the words from inside the building.

* * *

Reporting on all these activities were women journalists at the *Courier*, the *Chicago Defender*, and other Black newspapers. The *Courier*'s newsroom in Pittsburgh buzzed with activity as Edna Chappell McKenzie and Evelyn Cunningham documented and exposed the scope of lynching in surprising areas of the country in the South and beyond. Jackie Ormes was creating comic strips with Black characters who were independent and strong rather than the silly offensive caricatures of Black people in the white newspapers.

Another brilliant journalist, Alice Allison Dunnigan, was the Washington bureau chief for the Associated Negro Press, where Thompson had freelanced. She wrote about politics for 112 Black newspapers.

These women journalists went on to play other important roles as a driving force for the Black press and the country.

McKenzie and her team rolled out and publicized the Double V campaign. She went on to become the first African American woman to receive a PhD in history at the University of Pittsburgh and was then a history professor and activist.[12]

Cunningham, after 20 years with the *Courier*, had her own radio show discussing social and racial issues with such guests as Martin Luther King Jr. and Malcolm X. She then was a special assistant, first for baseball great Jackie Robinson, then for the governor of New York, and finally for President Gerald Ford.[13]

Jackie Ormes became the first nationally syndicated African American woman cartoonist with her comics appearing in 14 newspapers throughout America.[14]

Dunnigan was the first Black woman accepted into the White House press corps. She later took a job in the Kennedy and Johnson administrations.[15]

* * *

The Double V clubs, led mostly by women, began adding the "Non-Violent, Good Will, Direct Action" approach to some of their activities. One group, the Double V Girls Club of Cincinnati, Ohio, gathered in front of the U.S. Employment Services office with signs to protest unfair government hiring. Other clubs organized activities such as picketing at department stores with posters saying, "Don't shop where you can't work!" and "Don't shop where you can't try on clothes."[16]

Inspired by the "Double V" idea, Juanita Jackson brought 2,000 Black citizens to the capitol of Maryland to calmly protest police brutality in Baltimore. According to an article in the *Courier*, "These people represented the masses—the ditch-digger, the dock workers, the mill men, the small shopkeeper, women from all walks of life—and yes, the church leaders and intelligent professionals who live with the masses and not above them."[17]

The governor listened to them for two hours as they explained that they wanted a new police commissioner, a Black judge, and more Black police officers, including women.

Jackson ended the meeting by saying, "This demonstration was born out of the desperation of the people, and we demand immediate redress."[18]

The governor said he would set up a committee to study these actions. Jackson replied that by "immediate," they meant "next week, not next month or next year."

Juanita Jackson later led a citywide "Register and Vote Campaign," getting 11,000 more Black citizens registered to vote in Baltimore. She didn't want to wait for the governor's committee to act. She wanted to vote him out of office. That didn't happen in that election, but she kept on fighting.

Another action, organized by a woman law student named Pauli Murray, happened on a Saturday in spring of 1943.[19] Three Black students, men and women,[20] from Howard University, an all-Black college, entered a "whites only" restaurant in Washington, D.C., and asked for service. When they were refused, they sat down at a table; brought out books, pens, and paper; and quietly began to study. Police arrived but did not enter the restaurant, as the students were doing nothing illegal. Another three students came in and asked for service, again were refused, sat down at another table, and pulled out their books. Black students continued to enter the restaurant in groups of three until most of the seats were filled with studying Black students.

In frustration, the owner closed the restaurant for the day. The students left but formed a picket line in front of the restaurant with more of the student group who were waiting outside. When customers arrived, the students, eight women and five men, explained the situation. Some white customers expressed support for the group's action, one saying, "I think it's reasonable. Negroes are fighting to win this war for democracy just like the whites. If it had to come to a vote, it would get my vote!"[21] Another said, "Well now, isn't that something! I eat here regularly, and I don't care who else eats here. All I want is to eat. I want the place to stay open. After all, we're all human."[22]

The next Monday, the students were back picketing. After two days of this, the restaurant owner gave in, changed his policy, took down the "whites only" sign, and reopened his restaurant.

Pauli Murray and these students had just staged the first nationally recognized sit-in. More such sit-ins were held in other cities throughout the summer. Pauli Murray went on to become a powerful activist and friend of Eleanor Roosevelt, and sit-ins became a crucial tactic in the civil rights movement and beyond.

Layle Lane, E. Pauline Myers, Mary McLeod Bethune, Pauli Murray, and these others are just a few examples of the importance of Black women in fighting racial discrimination at home and abroad during the war. They developed a new approach with active nonviolent protests and sit-ins. These new tactics not only led to changes then but also moved the dial forward to be ready for the larger civil rights movement in the next two decades.

CHAPTER THIRTEEN

Slow but Steady Progress

"Navy Names 12 Ensigns; 1 Warrant Officer"

Washington—A spokesman for the Navy made public here this week the names of [13] Negro sailors who have been commissioned to officer grade in the Navy. [Eleven] of the 13 were named ensigns and are to serve as deck officers and two have been named as warrant officers.
—*PITTSBURGH COURIER*, MARCH 25, 1944, 1

ON A JANUARY MORNING IN 1944, 16 UNEASY AFRICAN American sailors sat in the commander's office at the Great Lakes Naval Training Station in Illinois.

"Do you know why you are here?" the officer asked.

Silence. They had no idea.

"The Navy has decided to commission Negroes as officers in the United States Navy, and you have been selected to attend an officer [training] school."[1]

Just a statement. No "congratulations," no "this is quite an honor." But the men knew they were making history. They would be the first Black officers in the U.S. Navy.

How did the navy evolve from allowing Blacks only as messmen to training them to be officers? It took several steps. Two years earlier, President Roosevelt had asked Secretary of the Navy Knox to expand the duties of Black sailors to the General Service, which included all the navy service jobs other than those in the Messman/Steward Branch.[2] Knox was firmly against this. The president reminded him that the sailors could handle work as mechanics, electricians, and firefighters and still be segregated, which he knew was Knox's concern. He instructed Knox to implement the necessary measures.

Three months later, Secretary Knox announced that as of June 1, 1942, the navy, the U.S. Coast Guard, and the Marine Corps would begin accepting Black recruits who would be trained for the General Service sector.

Depending on who was in charge at the specific bases, however, many of these specially trained sailors were still assigned to labor or custodial work. Indeed, as of February 1943, two-thirds of Black sailors were still doing mess duty. At least the skills these trained men had acquired might help them get better jobs after the war.

At the end of 1943, there were still no Black naval officers, and it was beginning to reflect badly on the navy. Knox was still against it. The president was not pleased.

Knox's aide and speechwriter, Adlai Stevenson (who would later be the Democratic candidate for president twice), had a plan. He convinced Knox to change his mind by pointing out that the army was getting better-educated and better-disciplined African Americans because there was a path there for advancement. To keep up with the army, the navy would have to commission some Black officers. There were, he said, 60,000 Black men in the navy with 12,000 more entering every month. "Obviously, this can't go on indefinitely without accepting some officers or trying to explain why we don't."[3] Stevenson suggested solving the problem by commissioning "10 or 12 Negroes selected from top notch civilians just as we procure white officers." Knox agreed.

So now these 16 men were being trained to be officers in the navy. Although they attended an elite training school, they were segregated into separate classes and barracks. But they knew better than to show displeasure with the arrangement and risk losing this opportunity. Their fellow African Americans and history were depending on them. They were determined to succeed.

They studied late into the night, closing the shades to hide the light. All 16 passed their final exams with scores so high that they were ordered to take the tests again to prove they weren't cheating. They scored even higher the second time.

Thirteen of these men were commissioned and assigned to onshore duties. They were known as the Golden 13.[4]

There was no explanation why only 13 of the 16 Black candidates became officers. The navy possibly assumed that not all the 16 would pass their courses, as was true with white officer candidates. But they all did. Perhaps it was because Stevenson had suggested that 10 to 12 officers should be commissioned, and they didn't want to go much beyond that. In any case, as all these men were equally qualified to be officers, the three who were not commissioned never knew for sure why they were left out.

* * *

The army was training Black officers in larger numbers than ever before. But unlike in the navy, Black and white army officer candidates trained together. They ate, worked, studied, and spent leisure time together. And it worked just fine.

Even in the South, integrated officer candidate schools, the army's first experiment with integration, succeeded.[5]

But once commissioned, these officers were assigned to segregated units to lead Black soldiers. There was little chance of further advancement because of the Army rule that no Black officer could have a rank higher than the lowest white officer on the base. Still, Black soldiers much preferred being led by Black officers, who treated them with respect, so it was an improvement. The army was making other changes as well.

As the war intensified and more American troops were lost in battle, Black soldiers were needed for combat despite the army's reluctance.

In 1942, the army activated the all-Black 92nd and 93rd infantry divisions, which had fought valiantly during World War I. The new young soldiers added to these divisions were trained at an isolated segregated army base in Arizona. As combat soldiers were needed, the 92nd and 93rd were sent to Europe and the South Pacific to fight.

The Army Air Corps needed more pilots too. In Alabama, the famed Tuskegee Airmen broke down the barrier for Black pilots and air crews. Training African Americans to be military pilots began as an experiment that many thought would fail. But these Red-Tailed Pilots (their nickname because of the red tails of the planes they flew) certainly succeeded. The Tuskegee Airmen would fly more than 15,000 missions throughout the war, destroy 261 enemy aircraft, and be awarded more than 850 medals.[6] Quite a group.

On the ground, another famous unit, the 761st Tank Battalion, known as the Black Panthers, reached France in October 1944 to serve under General George S. Patton. He told them he didn't care what color they were as long as they

Among the first to enter action returning home.
NEW YORK PUBLIC LIBRARY

were there to kill Germans. "Most of all, your race is looking forward to you. Don't let them down and, damn you, don't let me down."[7] They didn't.

The Black Panthers went on to fight in 183 days of continuous combat, including the Battle of the Bulge and the Battle of the Rhine, and were credited with capturing 30 major towns in France, Belgium, and Germany.

But while these African American units, who often fought effectively with white troops, were honored by the French, they returned to segregated American army bases and little fanfare.

* * *

Secretary of the Navy Knox died suddenly in April 1944. James V. Forrestal, the deputy secretary, was promoted to secretary. Forrestal had come to believe that the navy's policies were not only immoral but also inefficient.[8] Changes in policy picked up speed.

Later in 1944, naval officials enrolled 10 more African Americans in its officer training program. But as an experiment, these candidates trained alongside white officer candidates and, when commissioned, became staff officers in the civil engineering, chaplain, dental, medical, and supply corps. By January 1945, there were 34 African American naval officers, and the navy was continuing to train more in integrated training centers.[9]

NAACP activist Roy Wilkins recognized that "there is more than a little indication that the Navy is making a sincere effort to give the Negro in uniform a better break. This does not mean of course that everything is rosy in the Navy. . . . But it does mean that the Navy is aware of some matters and is devising and following a policy of correction."[10]

Between the army and the navy, the number of Black officers increased from five in 1940 to more than 7,000 in 1945.

* * *

The employment situation for Blacks changed too. A year after Randolph's canceled March on Washington led to Executive Order 8022, demand for more factory workers in the defense industries—along with a more effective Fair Employment Practices Committee to ensure that companies did in fact hire all races—led to more African American jobs. From Goodyear rubber to Kaiser shipyards, manufacturing giants were increasing employment of African American workers. The Black workforce in defense industries rose from 3 percent in 1942 to

9 percent in 1945. Black citizens were finally (if temporarily) enjoying the benefits of the new war economy.

On the publishing front, things were improving as well. After Sengstacke's meetings with Attorney General Biddle and then Secretary of the Navy Knox, Black reporters were included in press briefings and got better access to government policymakers. They now had official statements to publish.

The army's relationship with the Black press also improved, and Black journalists were no longer totally banned from army bases. The *Courier*, in return, began to print more positive articles about the army.

And in 1944, Harry S. McAlpin, a former navy war correspondent and reporter for the National Negro Press Association, became the first African American reporter to be allowed White House press credentials.

The head of the White House Correspondents' Association tried to talk him out of actually attending an Oval Office press briefing, promising to share his own notes from the meeting with him. But McAlpin was determined to be there, and at the end of the briefing, President Roosevelt shook his hand, saying, "Harry, I'm glad to have you here."[11] McAlpin's coverage of that press conference went out to 51 Black newspapers nationwide. Three years later, Alice Dunnigan became the first Black woman to get White House press credentials.

These changes for African Americans during the war were definite improvements, if only partially successful. Slowly, things were changing, and Blacks had more and more opportunity to fight for their country. They were proving themselves up to the tasks involved in winning a war. These positive experiments with integration in the military and defense factories made it easier for the total integration of the military beginning in 1948 as well as for the civil rights movement to come.

CHAPTER FOURTEEN

The Short but Effective Life
of the Double V Campaign

"1942 in Retrospect Shows Gains Outweigh Losses"
James M. Reid, News Editor

This edition of the Pittsburgh Courier *brings to a close
a year that has seen the Negro in America make many
advances along the road to full citizenship—advances
in the fields of politics, economics, pressure technique and
fuller participation in all phases of American life.*
—PITTSBURGH COURIER, JANUARY 2, 1943, 5

"WE HAD TO THINK OF DIFFERENT WAYS SO THAT WE COULD
keep from being full of rage because we knew that would be
counterproductive. And so, what we used to do is to have a
symbol that kept us having a vision. And the vision was a
'Double V' victory sign. And every time we saw each other,
we'd give that. And that gave us courage and hope and patience
because . . . we had two wars to win. And once we finished the
war against the Fascists . . . when we got back to this country,

we would fight against racism. Now what that did was . . . that unified us!"[1]

These words from an African American soldier serving in a segregated army in Biloxi, Mississippi, and then Okinawa, Japan, reflect Black servicemen taking the Double V symbol and campaign with them all over the world to help them get through the war.

As we have seen, the *Pittsburgh Courier* began its campaign with a brilliant promotion in February 1942 that grew it into

"Backing the Attack on All Fronts."
CHARLES HENRY ALSTON, U.S. DEPARTMENT OF THE TREASURY

a nationwide movement. As we would put it today, it went "viral"—as viral as something could without the internet.

As months went by, the *Courier* printed almost 1,000 articles, editorials, photos, and drawings about the Double V. More than 200,000 African Americans participated in Double V Club activities, making it one of the largest organized groups of Blacks in the country. And the message of fighting two wars at once energized and inspired many more.

But most of this messaging about the Double V in the *Courier* happened in the first six months of the campaign. By July, the number of Double V articles and photos were dwindling, and by the fall of 1942, there were very few.[2]

The paper didn't mention to its readers the reason it was phasing out the Double V promotion, and it might not have been noticed by many. But it was a definite change.

Why had the *Courier* toned down its push for the Double V? Historians have puzzled over this.

It certainly was not caused by a loss of circulation; sales had gone up, not down. From a customer base of 141,525, sales increased a year later to 190,684: a 37 percent increase.[3]

The reduction wasn't due to government intimidation; that fear diminished after Attorney General Biddle's promise to the *Defender*'s Sengstacke not to close the Black newspapers. As *Courier* reporter Frank Bolden remembered, "The government pressure didn't cause us to back off. We welcomed it. It helped sell more papers when we wrote about it. The FBI agents came to the paper day-in and day-out and frequently went to lunch with the columnists and editors."[4]

And advertisers weren't leaving because of the campaign. In fact, in the summer of 1942, faced with a new federal "excess profits tax,"[5] large American companies began advertising for the first time in the Black press rather than giving surplus income to the government in the form of taxes.

Was it to improve Black morale? It did need improving in 1942. In fact, the Government Office of Facts and Figures was so concerned about low morale negatively impacting military performance that it called Black publishers to a meeting to discuss it. But in an editorial, the *Courier* found it "amusing to see these people (government officials) so panicky over a situation which they have caused, and which governmental policies maintain. . . . If the Washington gentry are eager to see Negro morale take an upturn, they have only to abolish Jim Crowism and lower the color bar in every field and phase of American life."[6] The *Courier* was reporting the low morale, not causing it.

Black press experts believe that the reason for the diminishing Double V in the newspaper was more likely the result of the benefits of the campaign already noticeable by the autumn of 1942. A *Courier* article on January 5, 1943, was headlined "1942 in Retrospect Shows Gains Outweigh Losses."[7]

The biggest gains, it stated, "have been made on the job front where the President's executive order [8802] and the work of the Fair Employment Practices Committee (FEPC) and [other government commissions] have been effective in breaking the bars against Negro men and women." It also pointed out the vigorous support given Black workers by the entire CIO, the largest union in the country, which in turn forced the AFL, the second largest, to condemn the practice of unions refusing to admit Negro workers.[8]

The article then listed headlines they had printed throughout the year reporting positive things that had occurred during each month of 1942. These ranged from improvements that had already occurred in the military by that time, such as "U.S. Marines Decide to Accept Negro Recruits for First Time in Their 167-Year History" and "Army Expands MPs to Include 3100 Negroes," to "Negroes Win Political Offices, Including Congressman" and "CIO and AFL Unions Drop Ban on Negroes."

They reported that Black farmers had started receiving the same government benefits as white farmers through the agriculture department. Black teachers in Florida had won their equal pay fight, and a North Carolina jury convicted whites on an attempted lynch charge. Even seemingly small local gains appeared; Chicago added three Black municipal judges, and Detroit got its first Black women streetcar conductors.

Also mentioned was that, despite the many advances during 1942, there were some setbacks. Large racial battles occurred in some cities, the army was unable to protect Black soldiers in uniform from racial attacks in communities surrounding the bases, and too few Black pilots were certified in the Army Air Corps. There was still much to do.

But weighing the pros and cons of 1942, the *Courier*'s editors felt that there were more gains than losses, which boded well for the next year. It highlighted "most of all a vital militancy on the part of Negro Americans for a fuller share in the democracy we are fighting to preserve."[9] This had been a major goal of the Double V campaign.

The *Courier*'s editors decided that it was important to tout these achievements in their articles and to praise the organizations making the changes to encourage them to continue improving.

The army noticed that the paper was printing more positive articles about them than negative ones. They began to allow Black reporters onto army bases. The *Courier* didn't stop pointing out things in the country that needed changing, but it made sure to give credit publicly where it was due.

Again, in the words of Frank Bolden explaining the Double V's short life,

> *What else could we do? We had knocked on the door and gotten some attention and so the editors said, "Let's concentrate on what people are doing." For example, why would I want to read about the Double V when people are already working in a war plant down the street? I wouldn't.*
>
> *These gains showed good faith intentions by the government and other people [those who owned war plants], and we should follow suit. In other words, the Double V was like a Roman candle. It flared up, it did its work and then died down. It wasn't the sole reason things opened up [in the armed forces and industry], but it certainly woke people up.*[10]

And African Americans stayed awake.

CHAPTER FIFTEEN

After the War the Fight on the Home Front Continues

"Truman Attack on Racial Bias Hailed"

"Discrimination because of race, creed, color, or origin is contrary to the American ideals of democracy." This ultimatum, issued in his significant speech before the joint session of Congress last Wednesday, served notice on the American people that our Nation's Chief Executive knows that many of us are being denied our constitutional rights. He also indicated that something should be done about it.

—*PITTSBURGH COURIER*, JANUARY 17, 1948, 7

ON FEBRUARY 12, 1946, ISAAC WOODARD, A 26-YEAR-OLD Black soldier, was honorably discharged from the army. Still in his uniform, he boarded a bus in Augusta, Georgia, heading to Winnsboro, South Carolina, to reunite with his wife.[1]

When the bus stopped at a small drugstore, Woodard asked the driver if there was time for him to use the restroom. The driver cursed and yelled at him for asking. Woodard argued back, then returned to his seat at the back of the bus. When the bus next stopped, in Batesburg, South Carolina, Woodard was ordered off the bus by the local police, whom the driver had notified. They accused him of being impudent and causing a disturbance. When Woodard tried to give his version of events, a police officer struck him with a nightstick. Woodard was escorted to the jail, where the chief of police repeatedly beat his head and eyes with his nightstick until he blacked out. When Woodard regained consciousness, he was blind.[2] He had survived the war only to be horribly injured in his own country after it ended.

*   *   *

Nazi Germany surrendered on May 8, 1945. Four months later, on September 2, the Allies accepted Japan's formal surrender. World War II was over six years and one day after it began. The troops were coming home.

But before the German and Japanese surrenders, America had lost President Franklin D. Roosevelt, who died of a stroke on April 12, 1945. After working so diligently for victory throughout the war, he did not quite live to see it. The country grieved.

Harry S. Truman had been vice president for only three months. Now he was suddenly president of the United States. He told reporters, "I felt like the moon, the stars, and all the planets had fallen on me."[3] Now it was his job to end the war.

*   *   *

In the next five months, after more death and destruction around the world, the war was over. Now President Truman

President Harry S. Truman.
LIBRARY OF CONGRESS

got on with managing the return of millions of troops and leading the country back to life after the devastation of war.

At least 900,000 of the millions of returning soldiers, sailors, and marines were African American;[4] full of new experiences, knowledge, skills—and expectations. Was Woodard's experience what they would find at home? Too often the answer was yes.

Returning Black soldiers discovered that, even though the positive experiments in officer training integration proved that Black and white soldiers could work and live together, the army's top officials were not ready to change their policies. African American soldiers returned to segregated bases.

As many job opportunities as there had been during the war, now civilian jobs were scarce. The defense companies no longer needed to produce battle equipment. They laid off hundreds of thousands of people they had hired to handle the expanded war workload. Returning white soldiers and sailors reclaimed many of the remaining jobs. Black men and women often were the first to be laid off as the companies cut back, based on a last-hired, first-fired policy.

Despite the problems that Blacks faced in the army, its employment policies were better for African Americans than those of many civilian companies. The pay was higher and included housing. Many soldiers had learned new skills and taken on new responsibilities, so their work was more challenging. And the soldiers were safer than they would often be in their hometowns. Thousands of Black soldiers chose to remain in the army after the war.[5]

Three-quarters of the Black military were from the South. Those who left the military often went home to face danger from some racist whites. The violence was less than after World War I, when the summer of 1919 was called the "Red Summer" for the wave of racial violence in at least 26 American cities.[6] But it still happened.

Seeing African American men in the uniform of the United States angered many prejudiced whites. They threatened and attacked veterans, like Isaac Woodard, who were just trying to get home to their families and their lives. Local law enforcement did little to stop it.

As hard as activists had worked to end discrimination at home, Jim Crow laws were still in place in the South. But returning Black veterans who had been fighting racism and fascism in the war were prepared to continue the fight at home. They joined the activists who had been fighting on the home front to rid America of its segregation.

What most people weren't expecting was that now the activists had the president on their side. Harry S. Truman had been elected vice president largely by voters in southern states who believed that he agreed with their racial philosophy since he had grown up in Missouri, a southern border state. Much to their surprise, Truman, as president, was appalled to learn that, once again, as after World War I, Black veterans in the South were being brutalized and sometimes killed while still wearing their uniforms. The horror of those attacks and the refusal of police and the courts to address them were major factors in Truman's decision to act on behalf of African Americans.[7]

* * *

When Isaac Woodard was able to leave the hospital two months after the assault, he wrote a letter to Walter White at the NAACP telling him about the incident. White made sure to publicize the attack through the Black press, on a radio show with Orson Welles (a famous Hollywood actor and producer), and at a big fund-raising concert. As the *Courier* reported,

> More than 20,000 persons contributed $22,000 at Lewisohn Stadium Monday night for the benefit of Isaac Woodard, Negro war veteran, who was blinded by a Batesburg, SC police officer last Feb 12. Heavyweight Champion Joe Louis was co-chairman of the benefit committee. Fifty entertainers gave their services to raise funds for Woodard, who hopes to open a restaurant.[8]

White also made sure President Truman knew about this case.

"My God," Truman said in response, "I had no idea it was as terrible as that!"[9]

When South Carolina authorities refused to prosecute the police chief who had attacked Woodard, the

Truman administration, pressured by the NAACP, filed federal charges, which they could do because Woodard had been wearing the military uniform of the country. Much to their dismay, an all-white jury quickly found the police chief not guilty.

The case went no further, but President Truman did.

He issued Executive Order 9980 on December 5, 1946, establishing the multiracial President's Committee on Civil Rights.[10] He tasked the committee with studying "how state, federal, and local governments [could] implement the guarantees of personal freedoms embodied in the constitution." He expected this committee to recommend concrete proposals to improve and protect the lives and property of America's historically vulnerable citizens.

The committee submitted its report, called "To Secure These Rights," to the president. Among the recommendations were an anti-lynching law, the abolition of the poll tax, and laws to enforce fair housing, education, health care, and employment.[11] The *Courier* rated this committee report the most outstanding news event of 1947.

Perhaps the strongest of the recommendations in the report was for Congress to pass new legislation to "end immediately all discrimination and segregation ... [in] the armed services."[12]

This was crucial, but would Congress ever pass such a law? A. Philip Randolph didn't think so. He wanted an executive order to end military discrimination. And he wanted it immediately. In fact, he predicted there would be demonstrations if the president didn't issue such an order.[13]

There were other complaints in the Black press and community that, for all Truman's good talk, he hadn't really done much to change life for Black Americans. The president realized he would have to take quick action.

He found that the proposal to desegregate the military was the only one in the committee's report that he, as president, could implement without Congress's approval; as commander in chief, he had the final word on the military. So a month later, on July 26, 1948, President Harry Truman announced and signed Executive Order 9981, stating that "there shall be equality of treatment and opportunity for all persons in the armed services without regard to race, color, religion, or national origin."[14] He also set up another presidential committee, chaired by former solicitor general Charles Fahy, to enforce the executive order.

But there was some confusion about what the order meant, as it didn't use the word "desegregation" or "integration." Army officials believed that there already was "equality of treatment" in their segregated units and bases, although there really wasn't. "Separate but equal" had almost never proved to be "equal."

At a press conference the day after his executive order, the president firmly clarified that he did, indeed, mean that the armed forces were to be integrated.[15]

Fahy decided the best way to achieve Truman's objectives was to work *with* the armed services to design the best changes in policies and practices rather than to issue directives to be followed. The navy and the air force had already become the most integrated branches of the service and continued to institute the new policy with welcome assistance from the Fahy Committee.

The army was a different story. That branch of the military still believed that segregated troops were the safest and most efficient arrangement, so the Fahy Committee worked with them separately to enforce the rules. It took the committee and a new war in Korea in 1951 to get the army to integrate its soldiers.

The committee spelled out the ways in which segregation hindered the army's efficiency. Fahy reminded the army's leaders that during World War II, thousands of army positions, spread among 198 specialties, went unfilled. No soldiers had been trained for them because there weren't enough qualified white soldiers. Even though there were Black soldiers perfectly capable of being trained for these specialist positions, army regulations prohibited doing so. And of the 106 army school courses offered to soldiers, only 21 were available to Blacks. Hundreds of thousands of African American soldiers were confined to labor and service

Walter White and A. Philip Randolph, 1948.
AFRICAN AMERICAN MUSEUM AND LIBRARY AT OAKLAND, CALIFORNIA

battalions when they could have been serving in desperately needed specialized technical capacities.[16]

Efficiency had always been the army's argument *for* segregation. But in 1951, with the army doubling in size in just five months of war in Korea to 1.6 million American soldiers, 12 percent of them African Americans, Army officials found that their policy of segregation was not working. The Fahy Committee was right. The army quickly integrated its units.

It had taken decades of strategizing and effort by the Black press and African American leaders and four years from the time of Executive Order 9981 to integrate the military. The positive policy changes continued, and today the American armed forces are considered the most integrated large organization in the world.[17]

The *Courier's* most important campaign was finally resolved. Its other campaigns would soon be too.

CHAPTER SIXTEEN

Ready for the Future

"JACKIE ROBINSON'S THE 'ROOKIE OF THE YEAR!'"

The bronze, broad-shouldered first baseman whom the Pittsburgh Courier *plucked out of a mass of candidates in 1945 as "the Negro player most likely to succeed in the Major Leagues" has been selected as "the Rookie of the Year!" He is Jackie Roosevelt Robinson, fleet-footed star of the league-leading Brooklyn Dodgers.*
    —PITTSBURGH COURIER, SEPTEMBER 20, 1947, 13

"JACKIE ROBINSON'S THE 'ROOKIE OF THE YEAR!'" the headline shouted. Another *Pittsburgh Courier* campaign had reached its goal.

It was September 20, 1947. The *Courier* was thrilled to report that Robinson, the first African American player in major league baseball in 63 years, was having a fabulous rookie year. Their campaign to get Robinson into the majors had succeeded beyond their wildest dreams. And more was to come. Two weeks later, they announced that Robinson and the Dodgers would be in the World Series.

Dodger general manager Branch Rickey took a big risk by bucking the system to include an African American player. And it worked. There was a ripple effect, and today, as we know, most sports include Black athletes.

Jackie Robinson's reaction to the Dodgers being in the World Series was, "Once, when I was at UCLA playing football, I dreamed of playing in the Rose Bowl. I thought that would be the height of my athletic career. We fought well, but we never got into it. And now, here I am, playing first base against the Yankees in the World Series."[1]

This wouldn't have happened without Wendell Smith, the *Courier*'s sportswriter. Smith wrote columns fighting against segregation in professional sports as part of the *Courier*'s campaign. With the help of Smith's consistent prodding, Branch Rickey signed Robinson in 1945 to the Dodger's Montreal farm team. For the 1947 season, Rickey signed him on as first baseman for the Brooklyn Dodgers.[2]

In a later interview, *Courier* reporter Frank Bolden recalled Rickey "was impressed with the All-Star East-West Classic game that Black baseball leagues had every summer in Chicago. When he saw those 50,000 in attendance, he couldn't get over that, because the Brooklyn Dodgers were going broke."[3] Rickey thought that having a Black player might increase the Dodger's crowds. And it did. On April 19, 1947, the *Courier* reported that the Dodgers were "packing them in" with 95,000 fans attending the four exhibition games before the season began.

"Rickey took [Robinson] into the leagues," Bolden said, "not because he was a better baseball player, but [because] he could stand up under that punishment."[4] Robinson had played ball at UCLA and had contact with white athletes and audiences. Rickey knew that's what it would take to get along in major league baseball.

The *Courier* also considered Robinson's UCLA history in choosing him. Jackie Robinson didn't just play baseball and football at UCLA. He was the first at UCLA to letter in four sports: baseball, basketball, football, and track.

Having a vested interest in Robinson succeeding, the *Courier*'s editors arranged for Wendell Smith to travel and live with Robinson for a whole year while the team was on the road. They thought it would be easier for two Black men together to deal with having to stay at different hotels and eat at different restaurants than the rest of the team in the South. The *Courier* paid Smith's way, and he reported on Jackie for the paper every day.

Robinson did some reporting himself. To avoid Black anger at the racist comments toward Robinson during games escalating to violence, the *Courier* started a column called "Jackie Robinson Says."[5] There, Robinson spoke to *Courier* readers, encouraging them to ignore the insults and remain calm as he was doing: to just enjoy the games and help him make the season a success, which would help them all.

* * *

As exciting as all this was, the *Courier* named Jackie Robinson being in the World Series the *second* most important news story of 1947. The *most* important story was the Truman Committee report proposing the desegregation of the military.

What became of the other campaigns? Robert Vann's first campaign to get African Americans to vote for Democrats, mainly to get Roosevelt and his New Deal into the White House, had certainly worked. Blacks still vote mostly Democratic in the twenty-first century.

Southern voters had been staunch Democrats since the late 1800s, still believing that the Republican Party was "the party of Lincoln," who freed the slaves. This made it difficult for antidiscrimination laws to pass in Congress. But during the presidential election of 1948, in reaction to Truman's pro–African American policies, a group of southern Democrats broke off to form a new party, commonly known as the "Dixiecrats." They lasted as a political party for only that one election, but after that, the South was no longer solidly Democratic. Some of these Dixiecrats switched to the Republican Party.[6]

When President Lyndon Johnson, a Democrat, signed the Civil Rights Act in 1965, a flood of more southern voters became Republicans. The political parties began to redefine themselves, and by the 1980s, Republicans had a firm hold on white southerners.

* * *

The *Courier's* campaign for anti-lynching legislation had begun in the 1920s. As reporter Edna Chappell McKenzie said, "What people don't understand is that lynching dominated life for Black Southerners."[7] Through the years, the *Courier* reported every incident of lynching it could find.

Reporter Evelyn Cunningham was known for risking her life investigating such crimes in the South. She had been bored with writing articles for the *Courier* about card parties and fashion, the sorts of stories women journalists often were assigned. "I want to do some serious stories," she told her editor. "Like the lynchings down south."[8] He agreed. The *Courier* spread the word about lynching around the country, educating many people who were not aware of the level of the problem.

In the more than 100 years since the campaign began, there have been more than 200 attempts to get a bill passed through Congress making lynching a federal hate crime.

Such a law would allow federal prosecution of the perpetrators of lynching and hold local officials responsible if they didn't deal with these crimes themselves. Finally, in March 2022, the Emmett Till Anti-Lynching Act was passed, finally making lynching a federal hate crime.

In the years leading up to passage of this law, there were questions about some of the wording and complaints that it was just a "symbolic gesture" since murder, torture, and violent assault are already illegal.

But, as author and columnist Theodore R. Johnson wrote in the *Washington Post* in 2021, a symbolic violent crime like lynching seems to need a symbolic law against it. It is so much more than murder and assault. The goal of lynching is to inflict psychological terror to enforce a certain racial social order that goes against the country's founding principles of equality and liberty. The symbolism of a federal bill condemning lynching would identify these crimes as the hate crimes that they are.[9]

* * *

The campaign to improve employment opportunities for African Americans made big strides beginning with A. Philip Randolph's proposed March on Washington, opening defense industry employment to Blacks and other people of color. Continued pressure by the *Courier* and others, along with the needs of fighting the war, grew the job opportunities for African Americans. This increase took a dip after the war with the return of the white soldiers and factories going back to making appliances and cars, not war equipment. However, through the following decades, great strides were made in the number and types of jobs open to African Americans, including president of the United States.

* * *

What became of James G. Thompson, originator of the Double V? He remained at the *Courier* and was in charge of the campaign until February 10, 1943, when he was inducted into the army. The *Courier* announced that he was stationed at the headquarters of the 395th Coast Artillery Battalion at Camp Davis, North Carolina, as a supply office typist. He was there for a year and a half and was then shipped overseas to serve in the India-Burma Theater.[10] While there, he was awarded the Soldier's Medal for saving an Indian boy and a Chinese soldier from drowning.[11] He returned safely after the war and was given an honorable discharge on February 6, 1946. James G. Thompson spent the rest of his long life as a journalist.[12]

* * *

James G. Thompson at 79.
CERELIA L. SMITH, THOMPSON'S COUSIN

And what became of the Pittsburgh *Courier* and other Black newspapers? They had made great strides during the 1940s and into the early 1950s fighting for Black civil rights, although they did not use that specific term. They grew in circulation and prominence and were recognized as an important force in the Black community.

But their success ironically led to their decline. The Black newspapers continued to support the growing civil rights movement, but by the early 1960s, their circulation and political power waned. The larger the civil rights movement grew, the more it was covered by mainstream newspapers and television. One by one, the weekly Black newspapers began to shrink, and many eventually closed their doors and went out of business. In 1965, the *Chicago Defender* bought the *Courier* and renamed it the *New Pittsburgh Courier*.[13] It is still around. Other forms of Black publishing and entertainment grew, such as magazines, movies, and television.

The Black press, A. Philip Randolph, the NAACP, and many others played important roles leading up to the civil rights movement. With the newspapers' wide circulation, many African Americans around the country became informed and inspired. The Double V campaign allowed Blacks to fight for their own rights and support the war at the same time. People in small and large communities joined Double V clubs and learned that even small groups could gather to call out unfairness and achieve change. Blacks began to explore nonviolent protest and tried out such techniques as sit-ins and organized marches. These activities, according to historians, made the Black community and its white supporters primed and ready when the fight for civil rights grew into a nationwide movement in the late 1950s and 1960s calling them to action.[14]

Appendix

James G. Thompson's Letter to the Editor

DEAR EDITOR:

Like all true Americans, my greatest desire at this time, this crucial point of our history; is a desire for a complete victory over the forces of evil, which threaten our existence today. Behind that desire is also a desire to serve, this, my country, in the most advantageous way. Most of our leaders are suggesting that we sacrifice every other ambition to the paramount one, victory. With this I agree; but I also wonder if another victory could not be achieved at the same time.

After all, the things that beset the world now are basically the same things which upset the equilibrium of nations internally, states, counties, cities, homes and even the individual.

Being an American of dark complexion and some 26 years, these questions flash through my mind: "Should I sacrifice my life to live half American?" "Will things be better for the next generation in the peace to follow?" "Would it be demanding too much to demand full citizenship rights in exchange for the sacrificing of my life?" "Is the kind of America I know worth defending?" "Will America be a true and pure democracy after this war?" "Will colored Americans suffer still the indignities that have been heaped upon them in the past?"

These and other questions need answering; I want to know, and I believe every colored American, who is thinking, wants to know.

This may be the wrong time to broach such subjects, but haven't all good things obtained by men been secured through sacrifice during just such times of strife?

I suggest that while we keep defense and victory in the forefront that we don't lose sight of our fight for true democracy at home.

The "V for Victory" sign is being displayed prominently in all so-called democratic countries which are fighting for victory over aggression, slavery and tyranny. If this V sign means that to those now engaged in this great conflict then let colored Americans adopt the double VV for a double victory; the first V for victory over our enemies from without, the second V for victory over our enemies within. For surely those who perpetrate these ugly prejudices here are seeking to destroy our democratic form of government just as surely as the Axis forces.

This should not and would not lessen our efforts to bring this conflict to a successful conclusion; but should and would make us stronger to resist these evil forces which threaten us. America could become united as never before and become truly the home of democracy.

In way of an answer to the foregoing questions in a preceding paragraph, I might say that there is no doubt that this country is worth defending; things will be different for the next generation; colored Americans will come into their own, and America will eventually become the true democracy it was designed to be. These things will become a reality in time; but not through any relaxation of the efforts to secure them.

In conclusion let me say that though these questions often permeate my mind, I love America and am willing to die for the America I know will someday become a reality.

JAMES G. THOMPSON.

James G. Thompson, letter to the editor, *Pittsburgh Courier*, originally printed January 31, 1942; reprinted April 11, 1942, 5.

NOTES

CHAPTER ONE

1. In the first part of the twentieth century, African Americans were called Colored or Negro.

2. George S. Schuyler, "'Make America Real,' Says Double V Originator," interview with James G. Thompson, *Pittsburgh Courier*, April 18, 1942, 5.

3. Patrick S. Washburn, "The Pittsburgh Courier's Double V Campaign in 1942," *American Journalism* 3, no. 2 (1986): 73–86.

4. Washburn, "The Pittsburgh Courier's Double V Campaign in 1942."

5. Schuyler, "'Make America Real,' Says Double V Originator."

6. Schuyler, "'Make America Real,' Says Double V Originator."

7. Schuyler, "'Make America Real,' Says Double V Originator."

8. James G. Thompson, "Cessna Aircraft Jim Crow Hiring Policy Continues," *Chicago Defender* (National edition), February 14, 1942, 6.

9. Schuyler, "'Make America Real,' Says Double V Originator."

10. Schuyler, "'Make America Real,' Says Double V Originator."

11. Stanley Nelson, *The Black Press: Soldiers without Swords*, documentary, PBS, 1999.

CHAPTER TWO

1. Excerpt from Roosevelt's speech to Congress, December 8, 1941, https://www.loc.gov/resource/afc1986022.afc1986022_ms2201/?st=text.

2. George S. Schuyler, "'Make America Real,' Says Double V Originator," interview with James G. Thompson, *Pittsburgh Courier*, April 18, 1942, 5.

3. PBS, "Jim Crow Laws," https://www.pbs.org/wgbh/americanexperience/features/freedom-riders-jim-crow-laws.

4. Excerpt from President Roosevelt's State of the Union Address, January 7, 1941, https://millercenter.org/the-presidency/presidential-speeches/january-6-1941-state-union-four-freedoms.

5. Excerpt from President Roosevelt's State of the Union Address.

6. Schuyler, "'Make America Real,' Says Double V Originator."

7. James G. Thompson, "Kansas Critic Comes to the Defense of Singer," *Pittsburgh Courier*, December 25, 1937, 12.

CHAPTER THREE

1. *Pittsburgh Courier*, "We Are Americans Too! An Editorial," December 13, 1941, 1.

2. Stanley Nelson, *The Black Press: Soldiers without Swords*, documentary, PBS, 1999.

3. Patrick S. Washburn, *The African American Newspaper: Voice of Freedom* (Evanston, IL: Northwestern University Press, 2006), 144.

4. Rawn James Jr., *The Double V: How Wars, Protests, and Harry Truman Desegregated America's Military* (New York: Bloomsbury Press, 2013), 141.

5. Mark Whitaker, *Smoketown: The Other Great Black Renaissance* (New York: Simon & Schuster, 2018), 170.

6. Nelson, *The Black Press*, Vernon Jarrett interview.

7. Nelson, *The Black Press*, Phyl Garland interview.

8. Whitaker, *Smoketown*, 156; Washburn, e-mail to author, July 23, 2019.

9. Ken Love, *Newspaper of Record: The Pittsburgh Courier 1907–1965*, documentary, 2009, https://www.imdb.com/title/tt1419648.

10. WQED, *A Beacon for Change: The Pittsburgh Courier Story*, documentary, 2018, https://www.youtube.com/results?search_query=a+beacon+-for+change%3A+the+pittsburgh+courier+story.

11. Nelson, *The Black Press*, Frank Bolden quote.

12. "Publisher Robert Lee Vann," https://www.pbs.org/blackpress/news_bios/courier.html.

13. Love, "Newspaper of Record."

14. Love, "Newspaper of Record."

15. Love, "Newspaper of Record," Edna Chappell McKenzie quote.

16. Nelson, *The Black Press*, Phyl Garland quote.

CHAPTER FOUR

1. Ken Love, *Newspaper of Record: The Pittsburgh Courier 1907–1965*, documentary, 2009, https://www.imdb.com/title/tt1419648, Frank Bolden quote; Patrick S. Washburn, *The African American Newspaper: Voice of Freedom* (Evanston, IL: Northwestern University Press, 2006), chaps. 5 and 6.

2. Andrew Buni, *Robert L. Vann of the Pittsburgh Courier: Politics and Black Journalism* (Pittsburgh, PA: University of Pittsburgh Press, 1974), 193–94.

3. WQED, *A Beacon for Change: The Pittsburgh Courier Story*, documentary, 2018; "Publisher Robert Lee Vann," https://www.pbs.org/blackpress/newsbios/courier.html.

4. Stanley Nelson, *The Black Press: Soldiers without Swords*, documentary, PBS, 1999.

5. Love, *Newspaper of Record*.

6. "Publisher Robert Lee Vann," https://www.pbs.org/blackpress/news_bios/courier.html.

7. Nelson, *The Black Press*, Edna Chappell McKenzie quote.

8. Love, *Newspaper of Record*; Washburn, *The African American Newspaper*, 145.

9. Nelson, *The Black Press*.

10. Excerpt from James G. Thompson's letter to the editor "Should I Sacrifice to Live 'Half-American?'" *Pittsburgh Courier*, January 31, 1942.

11. Nelson, *The Black Press*, Edna Chappell McKenzie quote.

CHAPTER FIVE

1. James G. Thompson, "Cessna Aircraft Jim Crow Hiring Policy Continues," *Chicago Defender* (National edition), February 14, 1942, 6.

2. Five cents sounds like so little now, but, to put it in perspective, it was a 12.5 percent raise on their 40-cent-per-hour salary they were requesting.

3. George S. Schuyler, "'Make America Real,' Says Double V Originator," interview with James G. Thompson, *Pittsburgh Courier*, April 18, 1942.

4. Schuyler, "Make America Real,' Says Double V Originator."

5. Ronald Takaki, *Double Victory: A Multicultural History of America in World War II* (Boston: Little, Brown, 2000), 39; Cheryl Mullenbach, *Double Victory: How African American Women Broke Race and Gender Barriers to Help Win World War II* (Chicago: Chicago Review Press, 2013), 45; Rawn James Jr., *The Double V: How Wars, Protests, and Harry Truman Desegregated America's Military* (New York: Bloomsbury Press, 2013), 125.

6. Ken Burns and Lynn Novick, *The War*, documentary, produced in association with WETA, Washington, D.C., 200; James, *The Double V*, 124.

7. James, *The Double V*, 124.

8. Joe William Trotter Jr., *From a Raw Deal to a New Deal: African Americans 1929–1945* (New York: Oxford University Press, 1996), 90.

9. Trotter, *From a Raw Deal to a New Deal*, 89.

10. Andrea Davis Pinkney and Brian Pinkney, *Hand in Hand: Ten Black Men Who Changed America* (New York: Disney, Jump at the Sun Books, 2012), 96.

11. *Pittsburgh Courier*, "That March on Washington," editorial, June 14, 1941.

12. John H. Bracey Jr. and August Meier, "Allies or Adversaries: The NAACP, A. Philip Randolph and the 1941 March on Washington," *Georgia Historical Quarterly* 75, no. 1 (Spring 1991): 6.

13. Trotter, *From a Raw Deal to a New Deal*, 102.

14. Trotter, *From a Raw Deal to a New Deal*, 102.

15. A. Philip Randolph, "Defense Rotten," *Pittsburgh Courier*, January 25, 1941, 13.

16. "Randolph, "Defense Rotten."

17. Mullenbach, *Double Victory*, 46.

18. Copy of actual letter from Randolph to White, available at https://www.loc.gov/static/classroom-materials/naacp-a-century-in-the-fight-for-freedom/documents/randolph.pdf.

19. *Baltimore Afro-American*, May 10, 1941.

20. *Baltimore Afro-American*, May 10, 1941.

21. *Pittsburgh Courier*, editorial page, May 24, 1941.

22. James, *The Double V*, 124; *Chicago Defender*, "The Randolph Plan," March 15, 1941.

Chapter Six

1. *New York Amsterdam Star-News*, "10,000 Marchers Planned to Attend from New York City Alone," May 31, 1941; Rawn James Jr., *The Double V: How Wars, Protests, and Harry Truman Desegregated America's Military* (New York: Bloomsbury Press, 2013), 124.

2. *Baltimore Afro-American*, May 10, 1941.

3. *Baltimore Afro-American*, "Let No Black Man Be Afraid," March 15, 1941.

4. A. Philip Randolph, "Let the Negro Masses Speak," *New York Amsterdam Star-News*, April 12, 1941, 17.

5. Randolph's letters to Roosevelt and others, in John H. Bracey Jr. and August Meier, "Allies or Adversaries: The NAACP, A. Philip Randolph and the 1941 March on Washington," *Georgia Historical Quarterly* 75, no. 1 (Spring 1991): 10.

6. *New York Amsterdam Star-News*, "First Lady Is Not for Hike to Capital," June 21, 1941.

7. Bracey and Meier, "Allies or Adversaries."

8. Bracey and Meier, "Allies or Adversaries."

9. *Pittsburgh Courier*, "That March on Washington," June 14, 1941, 6.

10. Doris Kearns Goodwin, *No Ordinary Time* (New York: Simon & Schuster, 1994), 251.

11. *New York Amsterdam Star-News*, "President Roosevelt Orders Jim Crow Ban," June 21, 1941.

12. Jervis Anderson, *A. Philip Randolph: A Biographical Portrait* (Berkeley: University of California Press, 1986), 256–57.

13. Anderson, *A. Philip Randolph*, 256–57.

14. *Chicago Defender,* June 14, 1941, 3.

15. Anderson, *A. Philip Randolph,* 256–57.

16. "Prohibition of Discrimination in the Defense Industry" (from Executive Order 8802).

17. *Atlanta Daily World,* "Washington March Postponed," June 28, 1941.

18. A. Philip Randolph, "Wait, Watch Check," *Atlanta Daily World,* June 29, 1941, radio broadcast of Randolph.

19. *Pittsburgh Courier,* "Postponed," editorial, July 5, 1941.

20. Bracey and Meier, "Allies or Adversaries."

21. Bracey and Meier, "Allies or Adversaries."

22. National Public Radio, "The March on Washington at 50," *All Things Considered,* August 2015, https://www.npr.org/series/213897602/the-march-on-washington-at-50.

CHAPTER SEVEN

1. Rawn James Jr., *The Double V: How Wars, Protests, and Harry Truman Desegregated America's Military* (New York, Bloomsbury Press, 2013), 129–31.

2. Stanley Nelson, *The Black Press: Soldiers without Swords,* documentary, PBS, 1999, quote from Frank Bolden.

3. Nelson, *Soldiers without Swords.*

4. *Pittsburgh Courier,* "Messman Hero Identified," March 14, 1942, 1.

5. James, *The Double V,* 131.

6. Paul Alkebulan, *The African American Press in World War II: Toward Victory at Home and Abroad* (Lanham, MD: Lexington Books, 2014), 49.

7. *Pittsburgh Courier,* January 3, 1942, 6.

8. Christopher Paul Moore, *Black Soldiers: The Unsung Heroes of World War II* (New York: Random House, 2005), 51.

9. Philip McGuire, ed., *Taps for a Jim Crow Army: Letters from Black Soldiers in World War II* (New York: Oxford University Press, 2012).

10. McGuire, *Taps for a Jim Crow Army,* 191.

11. McGuire, *Taps for a Jim Crow Army,* 104.

12. McGuire, *Taps for a Jim Crow Army,* 191.

13. McGuire, *Taps for a Jim Crow Army,* 183.

14. McGuire, *Taps for a Jim Crow Army,* 166.

CHAPTER EIGHT

1. Philip McGuire, ed., *Taps for a Jim Crow Army: Letters from Black Soldiers in World War II* (New York: Oxford University Press, 2012), 166.

2. Rawn James Jr., *The Double V: How Wars, Protests, and Harry Truman Desegregated America's Military* (New York: Bloomsbury Press, 2013), 91.

3. Steve Sheinkin, *The Port Chicago 50: Disaster, Mutiny, and the Fight for Civil Rights* (New York: Roaring Brook Press, 2014), 10–11.

4. James, *The Double V*, 144.

5. James, *The Double V*, 29.

6. James, *The Double V*, 98.

7. McGuire, *Taps for a Jim Crow Army*, 184.

8. James, *The Double V*, 147.

9. *Pittsburgh Courier*, January 24, 1942.

10. *Pittsburgh Courier*, January 24, 1942.

11. James, *The Double V*, 147.

12. James, *The Double V*, 147.

13. McGuire, *Taps for a Jim Crow Army*, 186.

14. McGuire, *Taps for a Jim Crow Army*, 186.

15. McGuire, *Taps for a Jim Crow Army*, 186.

16. McGuire, *Taps for a Jim Crow Army*, 187.

17. McGuire, *Taps for a Jim Crow Army*, 187.

CHAPTER NINE

1. James G. Thompson, "Should I Sacrifice to Live 'Half-American?'" *Pittsburgh Courier*, January 31, 1942, 3.

2. "Editor's Note," *Pittsburgh Courier*, January 31, 1942, 3.

3. *Pittsburgh Courier*, February 7, 1942, 1.

4. *Pittsburgh Courier*, February 14, 1942, 1.

5. James G. Thompson, "Letter to the Editor," *Pittsburgh Courier*, February 21, 1942, 2.

6. Patrick S. Washburn, "The Pittsburgh Courier's Double V Campaign in 1942," *American Journalism* 3, no. 2 (1986): 73–86.

7. Washburn, "The Pittsburgh Courier's Double V Campaign in 1942."

8. Mark Whitaker, *Smoketown: The Other Great Black Renaissance* (New York: Simon & Schuster, 2018), 173.

9. Edgar T. Rouzeau, "Prejudice an Enemy of Democracy," *Pittsburgh Courier*, February 7, 1942, 5.

10. George S. Schuyler, "The World Today," *Pittsburgh Courier*, February 14, 1942, 1.

11. *Pittsburgh Courier*, February 14, 1942, 11.

12. Washburn, "The Pittsburgh Courier's Double V Campaign in 1942."

13. *Pittsburgh Courier*, "Ink Spots Added to Double V Honor Roll," July 11, 1942, 15.

14. *Pittsburgh Courier*, "Jimmie Lunceford Supports Couriers 'Double V' Drive," March 14, 1942, 20.

15. Washburn, "The Pittsburgh Courier's Double V Campaign in 1942."
16. Washburn, "The Pittsburgh Courier's Double V Campaign in 1942."

Chapter Ten

1. Patrick S. Washburn, *A Question of Sedition: The Federal Government's Investigation of the Black Press during World War II* (New York: Oxford University Press, 1986), 11.
2. Washburn, *A Question of Sedition*, 56.
3. Stanley Nelson, *The Black Press: Soldiers without Swords*, documentary, PBS, 1999.
4. *Pittsburgh Courier*, editorial, May 2, 1942, 6.
5. Washburn, *A Question of Sedition*, 49.
6. Washburn, *A Question of Sedition*, 50.
7. Nelson, *The Black Press*, Patrick Washburn quote.
8. Nelson, *The Black Press*.
9. Nelson, *The Black Press*.
10. Washburn, *Sedition*, 127; Mark Whitaker, *Smoketown: The Other Great Black Renaissance* (New York: Simon & Schuster, 2018), 174.
11. Nelson, *The Black Press*, Frank Bolden quote.
12. Washburn, *A Question of Sedition*, 73.
13. Washburn, *A Question of Sedition*, 89–91, including information from Washburn's interview with Sengstacke, April 21, 1983.
14. Washburn, *A Question of Sedition*, 89–91, including information from Washburn's interview with Sengstacke, April 21, 1983.

Chapter Eleven

1. Larry Tye, *Rising from the Rails: Pullman Porters and the Making of the Black Middle Class* (New York: Picador, 2004), 23.
2. Tye, *Rising from the Rails*, 79–81.
3. Ervin Dyer, "Porters' 'Underground Railroad' Carried Pittsburgh Courier into the South," February 24, 2002, http://old.post-gazette.com/lifestyle/20020224pullmanside0224fnp3.asp.
4. Tye, *Rising from the Rails*, xiv.
5. Tye, *Rising from the Rails*, 2.
6. Tye, *Rising from the Rails*, 83.
7. Allissa Richardson, "The Platform: How Pullman Porters Used Railways to Engage in Networked Journalism," *Journalism Studies* 17 (2016): 398–414.
8. Dyer, "Porters' 'Underground Railroad' Carried Pittsburgh Courier into the South."

9. Tye, *Rising from the Rails*, 83.

10. Dyer, "Porters' 'Underground Railroad' Carried Pittsburgh Courier into the South."

11. Dyer, "Porters' 'Underground Railroad' Carried Pittsburgh Courier into the South"; Ken Love, "Newspaper of Record: The Pittsburgh Courier 1907–1965," 2009, https://www.imdb.com/title/tt1419648.

12. Patrick Washburn, *The African American Newspaper: Voice of Freedom* (Evanston, IL: Northwestern University Press, 2006), 97; Dyer, "Porters' 'Underground Railroad' Carried Pittsburgh Courier into the South."

13. Interview with Earnest L. Perry, associate dean of graduate studies and research, Missouri School of Journalism, African American expert on the Black press, July 14, 2021.

Chapter Twelve

1. Cheryl Mullenbach, *Double Victory: How African American Women Broke Race and Gender Barriers to Help Win World War II* (Chicago: Chicago Review Press, 2013), 94.

2. Mullenbach, *Double Victory*, 94.

3. Mullenbach, *Double Victory*, 88.

4. Mullenbach, *Double Victory*, 45.

5. Author interview with Betty Reid Soskin, November 2, 2019.

6. Mullenbach, *Double Victory*, 45.

7. Mullenbach, *Double Victory*, 45.

8. Mullenbach, *Double Victory*, 52.

9. Mullenbach, *Double Victory*, 66, 88, 50.

10. Mullenbach, *Double Victory*, 51.

11. *Pittsburgh Courier*, June 27, 1942, 5.

12. V. P. Franklin, "In Memoriam: Edna Beatrice Chappell McKenzie, Ph.D.," *Journal of African American History* 90, no. 3 (2005), https://www.journals.uchicago.edu/doi/abs/10.1086/JAAHv90n3p345?journalCode=jaah.

13. Yoanna Hoskins, "Evelyn Cunningham Was a True Trailblazer in the Field of Journalism," *Simpson Street Free Press*, http://simpsonstreetfreepress.org/black-women-journalists.

14. Nancy Goldstein, *Jackie Ormes: The First African American Woman Cartoonist* (Ann Arbor: University of Michigan Press, 2019), review, https://aalbc.com/authors/author.php?author_name=Jackie+Ormes.

15. Jesse J. Holland, "First Black Female White House Reporter Gets Newseum Statue," *New Pittsburgh Courier*, September 24, 2018, https://newpittsburghcourier.com/2018/09/24/first-black-female-white-house-reporter-gets-newseum-statue.

16. Mullenbach, *Double Victory*, 63; *Chicago Defender* (National edition), "Women Protest USES Job Bias in Cincinnati," December 11, 1943, 7.

17. James M. Reid, "Thousands in Protest Parade: Md. Citizens Stage March on Capital," *Pittsburgh Courier*, May 2, 1942, 1.

18. Mullenbach, *Double Victory*, 35.

19. Maureen Honey, ed., *Bitter Fruit: African American Women in World War II* (Columbia: University of Missouri Press, 1999), 202, 273–79; Mullenbach, *Double Victory*, 57.

20. Honey, *Bitter Fruit*, 17.

21. Harry McAlpin, "Howard Students Picket Jim Crow Restaurant," *Defender* Washington Bureau, *Chicago Defender* (National edition), April 24, 1943, 5.

22. "McAlpin, "Howard Students Picket Jim Crow Restaurant," 5.

CHAPTER THIRTEEN

1. Dan C. Goldberg, *The Golden 13: How Black Men Won the Right to Wear Navy Gold* (Boston: Beacon Press, 2020), 6.

2. African Americans in General Service, 1942, https://www.history.navy.mil/browse-by-topic/wars-conflicts-and-operations/world-war-ii/1942/manning-the-us-navy/african-americans-in-general-service--1942.html.

3. Goldberg, *The Golden 13*, 150.

4. *Pittsburgh Courier*, "Navy Names 12 Ensigns; 2 Warrant Officers," March 25, 1944, 1.

5. Rawn James Jr., *The Double V: How Wars, Protests, and Harry Truman Desegregated America's Military* (New York: Bloomsbury Press, 2013), 154.

6. Walt Napier, "A Short History of Segregation in the Armed Forces," July 1, 2021, 5, https://www.af.mil/News/Commentaries/Display/Article/2676311/a-short-history-of-integration-in-the-us-armed-forces.

7. Napier, "A Short History of Segregation in the Armed Forces," 6.

8. James, *Double V*, 187.

9. James, *Double V*, 183.

10. James, *Double V*, 183.

11. The Arthur Ashe Legacy at UCLA, "First African-American Journalist in White House Press Corps," February 8, 2010, https://arthurashe.ucla.edu/2010/02/08/first-african-american-journalist-in-white-house-press-corps.

CHAPTER FOURTEEN

1. First-person oral histories: Ray Elliot, "World War II: 'Two Wars to Win': The Double V Symbol Inspires the Fight against Fascism Abroad

and Racism at Home," http://www.americancenturies.mass.edu/activities/oralhistory/index.html.

2. Mark Whitaker, *Smoketown: The Other Great Black Renaissance* (New York: Simon & Schuster, 2018), 176; Patrick S. Washburn, "The Pittsburgh Courier's Double V Campaign in 1942," *American Journalism* 3, no. 2 (1986): 73–86.

3. Patrick S. Washburn, *The African American Newspaper: Voice of Freedom* (Evanston, IL: Northwestern University Press, 2006), 161.

4. Stanley Nelson, *The Black Press: Soldiers without Swords*, documentary, PBS, 1999, Frank Bolden interview.

5. Patrick S. Washburn, *A Question of Sedition: The Federal Government's Investigation of the Black Press during World War II* (New York: Oxford University Press, 1986), 133.

6. "Hysteria over Negroes," *Pittsburgh Courier* (National edition), May 2, 1942, 6; Washburn, "The Pittsburgh Courier's Double V Campaign in 1942."

7. James M. Reid, "1942 in Retrospect Shows Gains Outweigh Losses: Negro America Still Faces Many Obstacles Ahead," *Pittsburgh Courier*, January 5, 1943, 5.

8. Reid, "1942 in Retrospect Shows Gains Outweigh Losses."

9. Reid, "1942 in Retrospect Shows Gains Outweigh Losses."

10. Washburn, "The Pittsburgh Courier's Double V Campaign in 1942."

CHAPTER FIFTEEN

1. Bryan Greene, "After Victory in World War II, Black Veterans Continued the Fight for Freedom at Home," August 30, 2021, https://www.smithsonianmag.com/history/summer-1946-saw-black-wwii-vets-fight-freedom-home-180978538.

2. Chris Lamb, "The Blinding of a WWII Vet Opened America's Eyes to the Evil of Jim Crow," September 9, 2019, https://www.navytimes.com/news/your-navy/2019/11/09/the-blinding-of-a-wwii-vet-opened-americas-eyes-to-the-evil-of-jim-crow.

3. "Harry S. Truman, the 33rd President of the United States," https://www.whitehousehistory.org/bios/harry-truman, https://www.whitehouse.gov/about-the-white-house/presidents/harry-s-truman/#:~:text=with%20Soviet%20Russia.-,Suddenly%20these%20and%20a%20host%20of%20other%20wartime%20problems%20became,Lamar%2C%20Missouri-%2C%20in%201884.

4. Greene, "After Victory in World War II, Black Veterans Continued the Fight for Freedom at Home."

5. Rawn James Jr., *The Double V: How Wars, Protests, and Harry Truman Desegregated America's Military* (New York: Bloomsbury Press, 2013), 209.

6. James, *The Double V*, 79.

7. James, *The Double V*, 227.

8. *Pittsburgh Courier*, "Batesburg Cop Admits Blinding Veteran," August 24, 1946, 3.

9. James, *The Double V*, 223; DeNeen L. Brown, "How Harry S. Truman Went from Being a Racist to Desegregating the Military," *Washington Post*, July 26, 2018, https://www.washingtonpost.com/news/retropolis/wp/2018/07/26/how-harry-s-truman-went-from-being-a-racist-to-desegregating-the-military.

10. James, *The Double V*, 217.

11. Library of Congress, "President Truman's Speech to the 38th Annual NAACP Convention," https://www.loc.gov/exhibits/naacp/world-war-ii-and-the-post-war-years.html#skip_menu.

12. Morris J. MacGregor Jr., *Integration of the Armed Forces, 1940–1965* (Washington, DC: Center of Military History, United States Army, 1985), 126.

13. James, *The Double V*, 226.

14. James, *The Double V*, 228.

15. James, *The Double V*, 229.

16. James, *The Double V*, 235.

17. James, *The Double V*, 240.

CHAPTER SIXTEEN

1. Jackie Robinson, "Great to Be in World Series—Jackie: My Greatest Thrill, Jackie Tells Courier," *Pittsburgh Courier*, October 4, 1947, 1.

2. *Weekly Challenger* (Tampa, FL), "That Time Jackie Robinson Was a Columnist for the Pittsburgh Courier," April 14, 2016, https://theweeklychallenger.com/that-time-jackie-robinson-was-a-columnist-for-the-pittsburgh-courier.

3. Stanley Nelson, *The Black Press: Soldiers without Swords*, documentary, PBS, 1999, Frank Bolden interview.

4. Nelson, *The Black Press*, Frank Bolden interview.

5. Jackie Robinson, "Jackie Robinson Says," *Pittsburgh Courier*, April 5, 1947, 14.

6. Becky Little, "How the 'Party of Lincoln' Won Over the Once Democratic South," April 10, 2019, https://www.history.com/news/how-the-party-of-lincoln-won-over-the-once-democratic-south.

7. Nelson, *The Black Press*, Edna Chappell McKenzie interview.

8. Yanick Rice Lamb, "Evelyn Cunningham: The Pittsburgh Courier's 'Lynching Editor,'" June 23, 2018, https://yanickricelamb.com/uncategorized/evelyn-cunningham-the-pittsburgh-couriers-lynching-editor/#_edn21.

9. Theodore R. Johnson, "Yes, Anti-Lynching Laws Are Mostly Symbolic. That's What Makes Them Important," *Washington Post*, October 29, 2021, https://www.washingtonpost.com/outlook/yes-anti-lynching-laws-are-mostly-symbolic-thats-what-makes-them-important/2021/10/28/6bd7feea-3744-11ec-9bc4-86107e7b0ab1_story.html.

10. The Personnel Records Center of the National Archives supplied the Army Post Office address for Thompson overseas as the India-Burma Theater, which was confirmed, along with his unit, in an article in the *Courier*.

11. *Pittsburgh Courier*, "Soldier's Medal for Ex-Courierite," November 17, 1945, 1.

12. Cerelia Smith-St. Claire, daughter of James G. Thompson's first cousin, Luther Daniel, Los Angeles, interview with the author.

13. Ulish Carter, "For 100 Years, the Courier Was There Leading the Way in the Black Struggle," *New Pittsburgh Courier*, October 22, 2010, https://newpittsburghcourier.com/2010/10/22/for-100-years-the-courier-was-there-leading-the-way-in-the-black-struggle.

14. Nelson, *The Black Press*, Professor Patrick Washburn interview.

BIBLIOGRAPHY

Alkebulan, Paul. *The African American Press in World War II: Toward Victory at Home and Abroad*. Lanham, MD: Lexington Books, 2014.

Anderson, Jervis. *A. Philip Randolph: A Biographical Portrait*. Berkeley: University of California Press, 1986. Originally printed in 1972.

Bracey, John H., Jr., and August Meier. "Allies and Adversaries: The NAACP, A. Philip Randolph, and the 1941 March on Washington." *Georgia Historical Quarterly* 75, no. 1 (Spring 1991): 1–17.

Brandt, Nat. *Harlem at War*. Syracuse, NY: Syracuse University Press, 1996.

Buni, Andrew. *Robert L. Vann of the Pittsburgh Courier: Politics and Black Journalism*. Pittsburgh, PA: University of Pittsburgh Press, 1974.

Burns, Ken, and Lynn Novick. *The War*. Produced in association with WETA, Washington, DC, 2007. Film.

Cooper, Michael L. *Unsung Heroes: The Double V Campaign*. New York: Lodestar Books, Dutton, 1998.

Delmont, Matthew. "African Americans Fighting Fascism and Racism, from World War II to Charlottesville." https://ibw21.org/editors-choice /african-americans-fighting-fascism-racism-world-war-ii-charlottesville.

Dyer, Ervin. "Porters' 'Underground Railroad' Carried Pittsburgh Courier into the South." February 24, 2002. http://old.post-gazette.com/life style/20020224pullmanside0224fnp3.asp.

Gates, Henry Louis, Jr. "What Was Black America's Double War?" https://www.theroot.com/what-was-black-americas-double -war-1790896568.

Goldberg, Dan C. *The Golden 13: How Black Men Won the Right to Wear Navy Gold*. Boston: Beacon Press, 2020.

Goldstein, Nancy. *Jackie Ormes: The First African American Woman Cartoonist*. Ann Arbor: University of Michigan Press, 2019.

Honey, Maureen, ed. *Bitter Fruit: African American Women in World War II*. Columbia: University of Missouri Press, 1999.

James, Rawn, Jr. *The Double V: How Wars, Protest, and Harry Truman Desegregated America's Military*. New York: Bloomsbury Press, 2013.

Love, Ken. *Newspaper of Record: The Pittsburgh Courier 1907–1965.* 2009. Kenneth A. Love International LLC. Film. https://www.imdb.com /title/tt1419648.

MacGregor, Morris J., Jr. *Integration of the Armed Forces, 1940–1965.* Washington, DC: Center of Military History, United States Army, 1985.

McGuire, Phillip, ed. *Taps for a Jim Crow Army: Letters from Black Soldiers in World War II.* New York: Oxford University Press, 2012.

Michaeli, Ethan. *The Defender: How the Legendary Black Newspaper Changed America.* New York: Houghton Mifflin Harcourt, 2016.

Moore, Christopher Paul. *Black Soldiers: The Unsung Heroes of World War II.* New York: Random House, 2005.

Morehouse, Maggi M. *Fighting in the Jim Crow Army: Black Men and Women Remember World War II.* Lanham, MD: Rowman & Littlefield, 2000.

Mullenbach, Cheryl. *Double Victory: How African American Women Broke Race and Gender Barriers to Help Win World War II.* Chicago: Chicago Review Press, 2013.

Nelson, Stanley. *The Black Press: Soldiers without Swords.* PBS. 1999. Documentary,

PBS. "Publisher Robert Lee Vann." https://www.pbs.org/blackpress/news _bios/courier.html.

Pinkney, Andrea Davis, and Brian Pinkney. *Hand in Hand: Ten Black Men Who Changed America.* New York: Disney, Jump at the Sun Books, 2012.

Richardson, Allissa "The Platform: How Pullman Porters Used Railways to Engage in Networked Journalism." *Journalism Studies* 17, no. 4 (2016): 398–414.

Schuyler, George S. "'Make America Real,' Says Double V Originator." Interview with James G. Thompson, *Pittsburgh Courier*, April 18, 1942.

Shaughnessy, Haley D. "The Double Victory Campaign and the Black Press." *Inquiries Journal* 7, no. 2 (2015): 1/1. http://www.inquiriesjournal.com /articles/1001/the-double-victory-campaign-and-the-black-press-a -conservative-approach-to-victory-at-home-and-abroad.

Sheinkin, Steve. *The Port Chicago 50: Disaster, Mutiny, and the Fight for Civil Rights.* New York: Roaring Brook Press, 2014.

Trotter, Joe William, Jr. *From a Raw Deal to a New Deal—African Americans 1929–1945.* New York: Oxford University Press, 1996.

Tye, Larry. *Rising from the Rails: Pullman Porters and the Making of the Black Middle Class.* New York: Picador, 2004.

Washburn, Patrick S. *The African American Newspaper: Voice of Freedom.* Evanston, IL: Northwestern University Press, 2006.

———. "The Pittsburgh Courier's Double V Campaign in 1942." *American Journalism* 3, no. 2 (1986): 73–86.

———. *A Question of Sedition: The Federal Government's Investigation of the Black Press during World War II.* New York: Oxford University Press, 1986.

Whitaker, Mark, *Smoketown: The Other Great Black Renaissance.* New York: Simon & Schuster, 2018.

Wynn, Neil A. *The African American Experience during World War II.* Lanham, MD: Rowman & Littlefield, 2010.

NEWSPAPERS

Atlanta Daily World, 1940–1945

Baltimore Afro-American, 1940–1948

Chicago Defender, 1940–1945

New York Amsterdam Star News, 1940–1945

INDEX

Page numbers in italics refer to photographs.

ABOUT THE AUTHOR

Lea Lyon is a published children's book author and illustrator. She is the illustrator of six award-winning trade picture books and one middle-grade novella and author of two picture books, one not yet released.

The picture books Lyon has illustrated or written address topical social issues, such as bullying, children with disabilities, and different ethnicities and cultures. The first of these, *Say Something*, by Peggy Moss (2004), about bullying, has, along with its 10th anniversary reissue, sold more than 80,000 copies. Her book *Lailah's Lunchbox*, by Reem Faruqi (2016), shows a Muslim girl successfully handling celebrating Ramadan in an American school. It was named both an American Library Association Notable book and a National Council for the Social Studies Notable Social Studies book for 2016 and was listed in articles in *Parents* magazine in 2016 and the *New York Times* in the spring of 2018 as an important book to be read for Ramadan. It has sold more than 92,000 copies. *Ready to Fly: How Sylvia Townsend Became the Bookmobile Ballerina*, is in the Scholastic Book Club and was released in paperback in January 2023.

For 10 years, as illustrator coordinator for the San Francisco/South region of SCBWI, Lyon organized and facilitated a popular annual children's book illustrator conference drawing 70 to 90 illustrators each year.

Lyon has an MBA in marketing. She worked in high tech as a product manager, including training various teams and rolling out a new billing system. Organizing and publicizing SCBWI conferences and workshops has made use of and enhanced her communication skills, analysis, computer proficiency, and effectiveness.

Lyon lives in Richmond, California.